KING
OF
Evanston

Book 3 of the Kings of the Castle Series

J. L. Campbell

Macro Publishing Group
Chicago, Illinois

King of Evanston by J. L. Campbell Copyright ©2019

MPG Ebook ISBN: 978-1-7331782-5-9
Trade Paperback ISBN 978-976-95586-7-0

Macro Publishing Group
1507 E. 53rd Street, #858
Chicago, IL 60615

Cover Designed by: J.L Woodson: www.woodsoncreativestudio.com
Interior Designed by: Lissa Woodson: www.naleighnakai.com
Editor: Lissa Woodson: www.naleighnakai.com

KING

OF

Evanston

Book 3 of the Kings of the Castle Series

J. L. Campbell

♦ ACKNOWLEDGEMENTS ♦

Special thanks to Naleighna Kai, the conceptualizer of the Kings of the Castle series, who brought together a wonderful group of writers for this exciting collaboration. Many thanks to J. L. Woodson for a fantastic cover. Thank you to my Tribe and fellow Queen writers. Much appreciation to Debra J. Mitchell, Michelle D. Rayford, Terri Ann Johnson, and Karen D. Bradley for your wonderful input.

Each literary endeavor comes with unique qualities. *King of Evanston* stretched me in several ways and reminded me that writing is about learning, growing, and expanding my horizon.

Many thanks to the Kings of the Castle Ambassadors, who have been a constant source of encouragement and inspiration. Shaz and the entire cast of characters are grateful for your enthusiasm.

In everything, I am reminded to give thanks. For health, strength, creativity, supportive friends and family, I praise the Almighty Father from whom all blessings flow.

ABOUT THE KINGS OF THE CASTLE SERIES

Books 2-9 are standalones, no cliffhangers, and can be read in any order.

Book 1 – Kings of the Castle, the introduction to the series and story of King of Wilmette (Vikkas Germaine)

USA TODAY, *New York Times*, and National Bestselling Authors work together to provide you with a world you'll never want to leave. The Castle. Powerful men unexpectedly brought together by their pasts and current circumstances will become a force to be reckoned with. Their combined efforts to find the people responsible for the attempt on their mentor's life, is the beginning of dangerous challenges that will alter the path of their lives forever. Not to mention, they will also draw the ire and deadly intent of current Castle members who wield major influence across the globe.

Fate made them brothers, but protecting the Castle and the women they love, will make them Kings.
www.thekingsofthecastle.com

King of Chatham - Book 2 - Reno
King of Evanston - Book 3 - Shaz
King of Devon - Book 4 - Jai
King of Morgan Park - Book 5 - Daron
King of South Shore - Book 6 - Kaleb
King of Lincoln Park - Book 7 - Grant
King of Hyde Park - Book 8 - Dro
King of Lawndale - Book 9 - Dwayne

CHAPTER 1

"Why do you think she's going to kill him?"

Shaz turned away from the group of teenagers who were using barbells and didn't need to be distracted. He waited for her answer as his stomach twisted. Camilla Gibson was going to give him a heart attack in no time with her reckless antics.

As he concentrated on the caller, he dabbed his forehead with the towel hanging around his neck.

"She's on her way to Alderman Bennett's office," Miss Mabel whispered.

"After I told her specifically not to do that." With his free hand, Shaz motioned to the boys. "Continue with your reps. I'll be right back."

The clanging of metal from various gym equipment filled the air as the young men followed his instruction. He stalked to the plate glass door, absently wiping away sweat that poured from his skin. When he addressed Miss Mabel, the owner of the Jamaican restaurant where he ate regularly, he lowered his voice. "I'm in the middle of a workout with the boys and I'm scheduled to have a session with them after—"

"I know they're important," Miss Mabel said, her accent growing deeper as her pitch climbed. "But dis is urgent, too. If ya don' come, I might have to kill ya."

"Why would you want to do that?" he asked, biting back a chuckle. Miss Mabel was always high drama, same as her niece.

"Because my sister might fly over from Jamaica and kill me after Camilla get herself in trouble."

Staring at the red brick building across the street, he said, "You mean more than she's in already?"

"Boy, don't joke at a time like dis." Miss Mabel's voice took on a desperate edge. "Ya comin' or not?"

Despite the way his gut twisted, an involuntary grin lifted his lips as he pictured her scowling. "Don't worry. I'll meet you there in fifteen minutes."

"Ya better make dat ten. The way dat gal behavin', she might be packin'."

The thought chilled his blood.

Camilla, Miss Mabel's niece, was in the U.S. accessing treatment for her daughter, who had a congenital heart condition. The little girl had gone through a series of tests and was yet to be scheduled for surgery. Camilla's visa would expire in just over a month and she didn't want to leave her baby behind and go back to Jamaica, especially since the treatment was not available there. Since Shaz met her four weeks ago, she'd turned his life upside down. This latest episode was a case in point.

He strode back to the teenagers, rubbing the hair on his jaw and chin. "Tajon, you're going to mess around and cause an accident."

The young man anchored the metal disc on the leg machine and raised both hands. "Sorry, Shaz. I got distracted for a second." He pointed to the flat-screen television anchored high on the wall facing them.

The teen doing leg presses grinned. "Distracted, my ass."

A sharp look from Shaz and Chris, who was spotting another teen on the bench press machine, had him mumbling. "Sorry."

Chris Deans, a dark-skinned giant of a man and Shaz's good friend, also volunteered at the youth club they started two years ago. They named it the Evanston Gentlemen's Club and used the facilities, adjacent to the community center, to mentor young men in and around Evanston and Chicago.

As he slid the towel from around his neck, Shaz debated whether he had time for a quick shower. "I have to leave, so you're handling the meeting."

"No problem." Chris tipped his close-shaven head to one side. "Trouble on the horizon?"

"That's what I'm trying to prevent."

In the locker room, Shaz grabbed his bag, then shot in and out of the shower in record time. He shrugged into a long-sleeved white shirt and a pair of dress pants he kept handy in his locker. At five in the evening, they were the only concession he'd make to this errand. Though his career as a lawyer demanded a professional look, he avoided being dressed to the gills as much as he could. He secretly hated suits, but preferred them custom-made for a better fit. Now, he rolled back his sleeves, re-tied his locs, picked up his bag, and left the building.

Five more minutes found him downtown, stepping out of an electric blue Alfa Romeo Stelvio SUV and riding the elevator to Darryl Bennett's office. The man served as an alderman and once wielded power at The Castle, a sprawling estate—a city within itself—where Shaz now had a seat on the board of directors. He and Bennett had had several run-ins, all of them to do with Camilla Gibson. Only God knew what he'd find when he made it to the office.

By Miss Mabel's account, Camilla was threatening to do the alderman bodily harm. After what he'd done, she'd be well within her rights to do so. But that wouldn't help her precarious situation.

If nothing else, the woman had chutzpah. Tall and slender, she was no match for Bennett, a strapping man who stood a few inches taller, and had a lot more to lose if things went south between them.

Bennett's office was elegant, with dark wood panelling and heavy sofas more suited to a living room than a waiting area. Shaz stepped around a table laden with magazines and addressed the alderman's receptionist. He'd barely said two words when Camilla's unmistakable accent hit the airwaves around him. "You're a damn liar. If you think

I'm going to sit around while you …"

A dozen steps took Shaz to Bennett's office, where he found Camilla stabbing her finger on Bennett's desk, while Miss Mabel clasped both hands to her bosom as if in prayer. When she laid eyes on Shaz, she mouthed, "Thank God, you came."

Standing to one side of Camilla, Shaz gripped her elbow.

She turned wild eyes on him as her nostrils quivered and her lips parted.

With a gentle squeeze to her arm, Shaz murmured, "Now that I'm here, leave this to me, please."

Pointing at Bennett, Camilla spat, "I don't care what arrangement he has with Derrick, he's not getting Ayanna."

Aside from a tic dancing around one of Bennett's eyes, the man didn't move in his seat. He threw a malevolent glare at Camilla before drawing a breath to speak.

Shaz put up a hand to stop him. "Camilla, Miss Mabel, please give me a minute."

After sending the older man a killing look, Camilla swept out with Miss Mabel on her heels. The black ankle-length dress, and her hair pulled into a top knot, highlighted Camilla's regal bearing. At the moment, she might look the part of a queen, but her attitude was far from that of a monarch. If Bennett knew what was good for him, he'd watch himself with this fiery woman.

The second the door closed behind them, Shaz said, "I'm not sure what happened to set this off, but—"

Bennett pointed to the door. "She needs to understand that I've made a *legal* arrangement with the father of the child. I have—"

"I don't care what you have." Shaz fixed his gaze on Bennett. "What I know is, you'd better put a hold on whatever funny business you have going on with Derrick Porter."

Bennett rose from his seat. "You can't come in here and tell me how to run my show."

"And you can't tell me you're so desperate to solve your family problems, you'd take advantage of someone who's here trying to find solutions for her sick baby."

Eyes wide, Bennett gasped. "You're just saying that. As far as I know—"

"You don't know anything, so shut up and listen."

Slowly, Bennett lowered himself to the executive chair.

Shaz folded both arms and held Bennett's gaze. "It doesn't matter that she came to your attention the wrong way, Ayanna Porter is *not* up for adoption. Nor will she be, in this life, or the next. Whatever paperwork or exchange you've done with Porter, consider it null and void."

Moving his head side to side, Bennett smirked. "Life doesn't work like that, Shaz."

"It's Shaz for my friends. Shastra for you. Matter of fact, Mr. Bostwick would be even better."

With both hands splayed on the massive glass-topped desk, Bennett grimaced at the insult. "I don't know what Miss Gibson told you, but my wife and I have a deal with—"

"You clearly didn't hear what I said." Shaz planted his hands on the half-inch-thick glass. "The deal is off."

CHAPTER 2

Under the dim light on Miss Mabel's matchbox-sized porch, Camilla stared at Shaz, defiance in her dark-brown eyes.

"I didn't do anything wrong." She stood straighter and waited a beat before continuing. "Especially since I don't know how that man could think I'm giving up my daughter for adoption. My situation may be bad, but I'm not that desperate."

"I understand all that," Shaz said, looking toward the street as a gold and black Stanley Steemer van drove by. "But I told you I'd handle it. You can't just storm into a politician's office and make threats. People get put into jail for stunts like the one you pulled this evening."

She angled her head back and shot a glare at him. "A desperate woman does desperate things."

They both knew she'd be deported and lose her visitor's visa if she overstayed the six months she was allowed to be in the U.S. and she was coming close to that point. Still, she was unrepentant.

"What exactly am I supposed to do when Derrick is trying to give away my baby?" she asked.

Moving his index finger between them, he said, "What *you* are supposed to do is let *me* deal with Bennett, and Derrick Porter eventually."

When she grumbled, he continued, "I know this is difficult, but you have to trust me. Porter has citizenship, so he has a right to be here. If you keep doing things like you did this evening, you can be sent home without your baby, or getting the help she needs. D'you understand?"

Camilla blinked and her eyes went liquid. Or so he thought, until she pulled her shoulders back and stepped away from him. "I know all that but I didn't feel I had a choice. If I leave, Ayanna goes with me. That means delaying the life-saving treatment she needs. And if you don't get a move on," she snapped. "I'll have to do just that."

Shaz winced, knowing there was more at work than she understood. He held her by the shoulders while studying her face. While Camilla's eyes reflected her frustration, her plump lips dared him to kiss them. He shelved that thought and focused on getting her to understand his position.

"Don't forget that with Dro's help we've pulled together more information than we had about your case. That will help us get to the bottom of this mess."

At the mention of his friend and fellow King, Camilla gave Shaz a grudging smile. "Yeah, he did come through on that, but—"

A car swept by and he released her, but lifted her chin with one finger. "Hey, let's take this one step at a time."

Ayanna let out a squeal from the living room, and Miss Mabel laughed.

Shaz tipped his head sideways. "You hear that?"

When Camilla nodded, her face in shadow, he turned her toward the door. "That's what's important right now. Go spend time with your little girl. Leave the business end of things to me."

She sucked in her breath, then lowered her chin as she expelled the air from her lungs. "Are you coming in to say goodbye to Aunt Mabel?"

Rubbing his jaw, Shaz hesitated.

With her head angled toward the living room, Camilla said, "She'll curse you out if you leave without telling her."

"I bet she will." Shaz motioned for Camilla to go ahead of him. "But I have to leave in a few."

A set of floral sofas positioned in front of a flat-screen television dominated the living room. At opposite corners of the space, a pair of standing mahogany shelves held family pictures and figurines in all shapes and sizes. A younger version of Camilla featured in some of the photos.

Miss Mabel sat on the largest chair bouncing Ayanna on her knees. The little girl squealed around the fingers jammed into her mouth. Her grand aunt dabbed her chin, then gave Shaz a grateful smile.

"I'll see you at the restaurant tomorrow," he said, easing his way out of the house.

Miss Mabel's gaze slid to Camilla, who reached for the toddler. "Ya leaving already?"

With his hands in his pockets like a guilty teenager reluctant to tell the truth, Shaz nodded. "I promised my mother I'd stop by and you know she doesn't like to be kept waiting."

"That's the only reason I'm letting you go." Miss Mabel said over her shoulder. "I have something for you. Give me a minute."

While running his fingers over the chain and pendant in his pocket, he watched Camilla and her daughter. The little girl stared into her mother's eyes. The delighted giggle and joyful pumping of her fists made it hard to remember Ayanna was seriously ill.

The affection radiating from Camilla's eyes hit him square in the chest and he vowed to do everything in his power to keep them together. He was about to tell her so when Miss Mabel came back into the room carrying a gold Tupperware container.

"Here, I cooked oxtail and beans today and I know ya love dat."

Shaz beamed at her, his mouth watering at the goods hidden inside. "I appreciate it. Thanks."

"No problem. Ya too tough." She waved one hand toward his body and cackled. "Ya need more meat on ya bones."

He laughed and took the plastic box from her. "You calling me stringy?"

"I say what I mean." Miss Mabel poked his arm and batted her eyelashes. "Ya too muscular. A girl needs some more flesh to fill up her hands."

On the periphery of his vision, Shaz caught Camilla shaking her head and biting her lip as though to keep in laughter. He winked at her and followed Miss Mabel to the door.

She went outside with him and whispered, "Thanks for coming. That man has a lot of power, so ya understand why I didn't want her to do nuttin' drastic."

"Don't worry. I spoke with him and her, so we should be good for now."

"Ya don't know Camilla." Miss Mabel's dark face screwed into a frown. "Just do what ya can as fast as ya can do it. *Before* her temper gets hold of her again."

He nodded and walked away, with one side of his mouth pulled into a smile. Miss Mabel's pronunciation of her niece's name left something to be desired. Whenever she got agitated, she dropped the middle syllable and ran the whole thing together into Camla. Her accent also waxed and waned depending on her level of anxiety and who she was dealing with.

As he sat in the SUV and switched on the engine, Shaz chuckled. Only Miss Mabel and his mother could get away with telling him the feisty things they sometimes did.

His phone vibrated and Paula Bostwick's home number showed up on the display. He engaged the Bluetooth and brought her on the line. "I'm running a little late, Mom, but I'll be there in ten minutes. What was so important though? I'm beginning to feel like a headless chicken, running from place to place."

"It's your brother." Her words carried no inflection, yet they conveyed an expectation that he'd automatically know what she wanted.

In a teasing tone, he said, "You have to be more specific Mom, since you have two other sons."

"Martin. Who else? Stop farting around, Shastra." She sounded more vexed than anxious. "If you don't get over here soon, I think your father and he might come to blows."

"Where's Roman?"

His mother had the habit of summoning them to the family home, forgetting they were all adults with their own lives. But when she called, they put aside whatever they were doing and made an appearance.

"Not here yet, but you know Martin listens to you."

Shaz had his doubts about that. More than anything, his older brother resented him. His grievance carried over from childhood and Martin hadn't matured enough to leave the past where it belonged.

"Let me get off the phone, so you can concentrate—"

Raised voices in the background interrupted her. In the silence, his father shouted. "You're not going to come into my house acting like you own it. If you can't act civil, I'll throw you out on your ass."

A crash followed his words. Paula ended the call without saying goodbye.

Shaz put his foot on the gas.

CHAPTER 3

"Camilla, I need to have a serious talk wid ya." Aunt Mabel sat on one of the small sofas and lowered the volume on the television that was tuned to her favorite soap opera. Despite her neutral tone, Camilla knew her aunt had serious concerns. Although Shaz left minutes ago, Aunt Mabel still hadn't taken off her wig. That was the first thing she discarded after work. Next came the bra, which meant nothing else would be done for the rest of the night.

Camilla positioned Ayanna on her lap, facing the television. The figures onscreen captured her attention and she stayed quiet, squeezing a stuffed rabbit to her chest.

"Auntie, I know what you're going to say, but—"

"What about if ya listen to me for a bit?" Aunt Mabel gestured to Ayanna, who was motionless. "Your baby is why ya come here. Ya need to remember dat. Ya can't just haul ya tail into a politician's office and threaten him. Dis is not Jamaica."

Camilla wanted to roll her eyes, but didn't. Auntie knew very well she couldn't have done that at home. But her fury had carried her past the alderman's receptionist, and her fear of losing her daughter gave Camilla the energy to tell him exactly what she thought of him. Plus, Auntie didn't understand how mad she'd been since she realized what Derrick had done with the help of that scuzzy alderman.

Things like this weren't supposed to happen to people like her.

Though the place was beautiful, dubbed the land of wood and water by the original inhabitants, Jamaica was now overrun with corrupt politicians. She expected better in the United States, the land of opportunity, where many Caribbean nationals aspired to live and work.

"Auntie, I know things work differently here, and I'm sorry, but that man should know better."

"Well *dat man* can make life very difficult for ya." She scratched her head, lifting the edge of her wig. When she pulled it down, it sat askew. "He can also find a way to make *my* life hell."

Camilla struggled to keep a straight face as Auntie Mable pinned her to the seat with a hard glare. "I don't know why ya thought it was a good idea to go there wid ya loud noise and disrupt di peace." Aunt Mabel paused to draw a breath. "And by di way, Stacey was late for work because you choose to fly out of here like one o' dem Taino Indians running from Christopher Columbus and him gang of flea-bitten sailors."

Aunt Mabel's reference to the indigenous Indians who occupied Jamaica before the Spanish arrived in 1494 and decimated them with diseases and enslavement, almost undid Camilla. Who knew her aunt retained all of that history from childhood lessons?

Aunt Mabel would have been annoyed if Camilla dissolved into laughter, so she bit her lip and put on a penitent expression. She *was* sorry she'd kept her cousin away from her job while babysitting Ayanna.

"I'm sorry about that, Auntie. I thought I would have been back in enough time for Stacey to get to the hospital for her shift."

"Well, she didn't." Aunt Mabel's expression was sour as if she'd sucked on a Seville orange. "Dis is not Jamaica where ya can be late for work and it don't come out of ya pay."

Now Camilla felt bad. "I'll make it up to her, but Derrick had the nerve to tell me on the phone that Mr. Bennett could help, as if I didn't know what the two of them are up to."

She moaned in frustration, wishing she had a magic formula to put things right.

When Ayanna copied her groan, an involuntary smile broke free. Then, Camilla scowled. "As if I asked him for any help." The memory of their first disagreement came to mind and she rubbed her eyes. Pity that wouldn't erase their short-lived history. "Only God knows what I saw in him."

"Since only God can answer dat question, let's get back to what I was saying." Aunt Mabel narrowed her dark-brown eyes. "The fact is, ya need to toe di line and sort out ya visa problem. Di last thing ya want is to find yaself on a plane to Jamaica, minus ya pickney."

Despite the way her heart rate kicked up, Camilla said, "Auntie that won't happen. I'm not leaving here without Ayanna. I'd rather die first."

"Ya hear 'bout what's happening on the Mexican border? Dis is serious business. Dey will do it and ya have no say."

Camilla shifted on the cushion, feeling as if someone had dropped a vice around her head and chest. Yes, she was acutely aware of what was on the news. She might think she was safe, but when it came down to it, the only difference between those migrant parents and her, was that—they came seeking asylum the correct way, though the current administration said otherwise—she had entered the country legally. If she didn't get her visa renewed soon, she wouldn't be in any better position than them.

"Auntie, I know, but Shaz is trying to work around my visa problem. Even though it seems to be taking him forever to get things straightened out with the alderman."

Aunt Mabel's eyes blazed. "I don' want to hear one bad word about dat man. He didn't have to take ya case. He did it because of me, and at a good rate too, as ya well know."

For a second, Camilla closed her eyes, knowing part of that *good rate* came from Aunt Mabel filling that man's bottomless pit on occasion, aside from the lunches he bought from her each week. "I know and I'm grateful."

"Ya sure don't sound that way."

Sighing, Camilla fixed her gaze on the television. "Trust me, I am."

Despite the deep discount he'd given them, only charging if any court or filing fees, Camilla's pocket had been feeling the pinch when it came to medical bills. She'd stashed away money from her time on the runway in Jamaica and the Caribbean. Since she started travelling to various places and writing about her adventures, she'd monetized her blog. Her following had grown by thousands each month and sponsors were still courting her, despite the fact that she hadn't been anywhere new in months.

The blog had shifted to more serious matters, including the crisis at the U.S./Mexico border and the worldwide impact of climate change.

Ayanna's doctor's visits, hospital stays, and previous treatment had been expensive. If the money didn't keep flowing in, she'd soon have to tap into her investment account, which she wanted to avoid at all costs.

The anxiety that had flooded her system for weeks, fled on an adrenaline high when she marched into Alderman Bennett's office and told him she knew what racket he was running to steal her baby. Now it came back and compressed her chest until she could barely breathe. She filled her lungs with air and let it out, telling herself not to lose her peace. Shaz's fees were a necessity. Critical, in fact. She'd been through many nerve-wracking moments and came through them with determination and help from Mom and Aunt Mabel. Things didn't look bright now, but she'd be okay. In time. But time was now coming up short.

"Ya look worried, Camilla."

Aunt Mabel's voice snapped her out of her mental fog. "A little, but worrying doesn't help, so I'm trying to keep an open mind."

At that point, Ayanna dropped the pink and blue rabbit. When Camilla didn't release her, Ayanna squirmed and fussed to be put on the floor.

Camilla set the toddler on her feet, and Ayanna grabbed the rabbit by one ear and squatted on the tiles, closer to the television.

"God will work it out. Him always fait'ful." With a wily look in her eyes, Aunt Mabel continued, "Meantime, ya just need to work wid di program since you and Shaz like each other."

"What program?" Camilla asked, suspecting her aunt already knew. The sparks that flew between them whenever that man came near, were enough to start an inferno.

"Well, him is a good man." All innocence, Aunt Mabel shrugged, but a sly smile played around her lips. "If ya play di right cards, ya could marry him and stay here. Then, Ayanna could get all di treatment she needs for as long as necessary."

Frowning, Camilla rose to get water for Ayanna. "Please take that out of your mind, Auntie."

Aunt Mabel pulled back her head and raised both eyebrows. "What's wrong wid Shastra Bostwick?"

"Nothing at all." She went toward the kitchen, speaking over her shoulder. "But I couldn't do that."

"I'm not telling ya to do nutten," Aunt Mabel snapped. "Di problem is ya have too much pride. Just like Edith."

"Leave Mom out of this." Camilla grinned as she walked into the compact kitchen. "She raised me right."

"I understand dat, but when ya desperate ya look for every way out." Aunt Mabel yelled after her. "Since I been in America, I clean house, work from di bottom at a Caribbean restaurant until I was di head cook. Meantime, I was saving every penny to start my own business. I couldn't go back to school because I had Stacey to take of, so I had to make things work. Ya have a chance at things being easier for ya. Dat's all I'm saying."

As she filled Ayanna's cup with the filtered water from the tap, Camilla's smile faded. The fairy tale Auntie just concocted with Shaz at the center would be a perfect ending to their story. Shastra was everything she admired in a man—decisive, steady, patient, and even more sexy, his name, which sounded strong and powerful. Just like the man himself.

Their situation wasn't ideal but she was falling for him as the days went by. She wasn't sure they were on the same emotional wavelength but if the way he treated her was anything to go by, Shaz was feeling her, too.

A knock on the door sounded above the conversation and sound effects coming from the television, which Aunt Mabel had turned up high.

Camilla's footsteps faltered as she remembered the heat and solid strength of Shaz's frame pressed against hers. The man was physically fit, not to mention handsome—with well-defined lips and a narrow nose, and that pale mocha skin. His locs were soft to the touch, in direct contrast to his rock-hard body. Making love with him would be fire. The thought of being in the same bed with him made her—

"Camilla." Aunt Mabel's demanding tone woke Camilla from her daydream.

She rushed back into the living room in time to catch Ayanna toddling toward the bedrooms, as though avoiding an unwanted visitor.

"Someone's here to see ya." Aunt Mabel pointed behind her as she passed Camilla. "I looked through the peephole. Lemme go catch dat likkle rascal."

Camilla guessed who was outside, by her aunt's dour expression, and stalked to the door to yank it open.

Ayanna's father stood on the other side. Going by his thunderous expression, Camilla figured he'd heard about her trip to the alderman's office.

He took a step forward, but Camilla held her ground.

"Haven't you done enough, Derrick?" She stood in the doorway, blocking the entrance. "You're not welcome here. And by the way, what the hell d'you want?"

CHAPTER 4

Shaz glowered at his older brother, who'd followed him into the back yard. "Which part of *what's wrong with you* don't you understand?"

Martin stood eye to eye with Shaz, scowling back at him. "I don't owe you any explanation."

"You do, when you come over here upsetting our parents."

Their mother was already in a snit because between Martin and their father, they'd broken a stack of her prized porcelain plates she inherited from her grandmother. If Martin knew what was good for him, he'd chill. Paula Bostwick didn't take crap from anyone, including her children.

Martin rubbed his bearded chin, mirroring Shaz's reaction when he was perplexed. "So maybe I was a little angry when I got here because of my blowout with Sondra, but—"

"That's no reason to bring your bad vibes with you."

Taking a step back, Martin asked, "Why does it even bother you?"

"When you disturb them." Shaz pointed over his shoulder to the house. "You disturb me. And Roman. And Denise."

Martin ran a hand over his hair and tipped one brow. "All of this over an argument with Father?"

"Yeah, you know the deal. Mom is calling out the cavalry once you and Dad knock heads."

"A little melodramatic, don't you think?"

"Not when you come over here spreading sh—"

Taking a step back, Martin folded his arms. "You're a little hot under the collar for what's par for the course around here. Seems you might have a little something of your own going on." He paused and studied Shaz. "Something you might not even want to admit to right now."

His comment made Shaz take quick stock. If anything, the gravity of Camilla's situation remained at the back of his mind since the day they met. But not enough to make him crabby. He shook his head. "Nah, man. Come again. The only thing putting a burr up my backside is you and the fact that you don't know how to handle your problems. Never have."

The crickets chirping in the yard were loud in the beat of time before Martin spoke.

"You know what your problem is? Because you've always been the favourite, you think everybody owes you an explanation." Martin's tone turned bitter. "Even for breathing, as if you're some kind of god."

Shaz didn't dignify his words with a response. His brother had had an unhealthy rivalry with him since childhood. All because of how they came to live in the United States. Because of the eight-year difference in their ages, their mother had made the hard choice to take Shaz—who was four at the time—and Denise, six years old, with her when it was time for her to join their father in Evanston. As the eldest, Martin and Roman remained in Jamaica in their maternal grandmother's care for two years. Martin never forgave their parents for the way that situation unfolded. At thirty-two, Shaz couldn't figure out why Martin refused to release the past.

"Shastra. Martin." Their mother called from the doorway. "Come to the table."

Shaz brushed past his brother. "We'll continue this later."

"Not if I have anything to say about it," Martin retorted.

Their mother stood square in the threshold. Nobody was getting past without her running interference. When they both stopped in front of her, she looked from one to the other. "I hope you left your squabble out there in the yard."

"Isn't that why you called him over here?" Martin huffed, running a hand over his close-cropped hair. "To get in my face?"

Paula turned smoldering eyes on her eldest son. "Don't get it twisted. I asked him to come over so Teddy wouldn't kick you straight into next week. You may have hit forty, but when you step into our home, you'd best remember your place."

She took a step back and let Shaz slip past her into the house. "Do you understand me?"

Martin mumbled something Shaz didn't hear before tracing his footsteps through the kitchen and into the adjoining dining area. Easing up to his sister, who laid a tray of jerked chicken on the dining table, Shaz tugged her ponytail and kissed her cheek. "Hey, baby sis."

Giving him a mock glare, she quipped, "The only baby around here is you."

They both snickered at their corny joke. Because of her diminutive size, Shaz had always treated her as if he was older. He took in her usual gear of jeans and shirt before asking, "What excuse did Moms use to get you over here today?"

Sneaking a glance toward the kitchen, Denise murmured, "None. She told me they had some news, so I was to come after leaving the shop."

Denise's place of business, All Our Children, was ten minutes away. She ran a combination salon and spa for kids and had five employees, which gave her the flexibility to appear quickly whenever their mother called—unlike her sons, who were engaged in sheltering humanity and saving the world, as she half-jokingly referred to their respective professions.

"Where's Roman?" Shaz asked as his father walked into the room.

Theodore Bostwick, a mature version of his three sons, pointed over his shoulder. "Just drove in. That boy is going to be late for his own funeral."

Everybody except Martin chuckled as they slid into the seats they'd held at the circular table since they were children. The familiar room contained two massive breakfronts, chockfull of glassware and cutlery. Some of the items, Paula shipped over from Jamaica after she landed. She was getting ready to say grace when Roman, with sleeves rolled back and his tie missing, slid into the chair between Martin and Denise.

After Paula Bostwick gave thanks for their family and the meal, she sat back watching them. Her black hair—threaded with a few strands of gray—was pulled into a bun, highlighting her unlined mocha skin. Her deep-brown eyes glowed with indulgence as they helped themselves to the finest food this side of Evanston. For a few minutes, conversation came to a halt while they concentrated on filling their stomachs. Roman broke the silence first. "You never fail to hit the spot with your jerk, Dad."

Teddy Bostwick inclined his head toward his wife on his right. "Your mama's rub adds that special touch."

Nodding, Shaz reached for a chicken leg but Denise swiped it first, then stuck out her tongue.

"Greedy girl," Shaz said, before settling for a wing and tipping one brow at his father. "So, Dad, what did you want to tell us? I hear you have news."

Theodore and Paula Bostwick exchanged a speaking glance before looking at each of their children.

"You might want to tell us before we think one of you is about to die from some terminal illness," Roman said after wiping his mouth with a napkin.

"Nothing like that," Teddy said, clasping Paula's hand. "You all know I've worked hard over the years to give you the best I could."

Martin shifted in his chair, which drew Roman, Shaz, and Denise's gazes to him. Each dared him to say one word. When he sat unmoving, their father continued, "We've put our all into building this business, so you could have something to call your own in this land of opportunity. All of you have done well in your chosen careers. The business is flourishing." His gaze briefly went to Martin, who'd been stubborn about working for, and with, strangers versus his father.

Shaz shifted in his seat when Theodore Bostwick's unreadable eyes met his for a few seconds.

"So," Teddy added, breathing in deeply, "your mother and I have decided it's time for me to retire."

"Are you sure you're not sick, Daddy?" Denise's well-defined brows pulled toward each other as she stared at Teddy, whose copper-toned skin had darkened over the years and was wrinkled from too much exposure to the sun.

He rested a hand on top of Paula's and shook his head. "I've never been in better health."

The silence in the room stretched while he studied each of his children. "Fact is, I've worked like a dog since the day I landed in this country."

Their mother murmured, "You all know that's true."

None of them could deny that fact. Teddy Bostwick had worked two jobs until he brought his wife and all the children to Chicago. The way their mother told it, Teddy denied himself every luxury to pay the immigration lawyer he hired. Then he and Paula scrimped and saved to start Bostwick Construction. Only after Denise and Shaz were older did Paula earn her qualifications and venture into the working world as a teacher. She believed, as did their father, that education was the surest way out of poverty and had instilled that belief in her children. Her Master's in Elementary Education supported her drive to achieve and prove to her kids what they could do when they applied themselves to excelling at whatever they did.

"Since you never relax, what are you gonna do with your retirement?" Shaz asked, after a sip of lemonade.

"Yeah," Roman asked. "Next thing I know, the two of you will end up in the news." He made two lines through the air with his thumb and index finger, imitating ticker tape. "Woman Kills Husband For Getting Underfoot After Retirement."

They all laughed, until Teddy cleared his throat. "Not likely. Paula and I are going on a cruise. Then we're going to spend some time in Jamaica. We'll be away for at least six months."

The blast of car horns and the cricket chorale were loud in the sudden gap that developed in the conversation.

Roman recovered first, running a hand over his shirt. "So, um, who's gonna run the business?"

One by one all eyes went to Martin, whose mouth was full of chicken. When he swallowed, he cocked one brow. "Why is everybody looking at me?"

This was not going to go well. When nobody said anything, Shaz hid a grin behind his glass.

"As they say in those high-school yearbooks, "You're the one most likely to …" Shaz let the thought hang while his gaze shifted to Roman and Denise, who watched him and Martin.

"As you well know," Martin said, laying down his knife and fork, "I'm busy."

"Yeah, busy building other people's dreams while neglecting your own," Shaz said.

"Nobody's all up in your business instructing you what to do, so don't try and tell me how to run mine." Martin picked up a slice of fried, green plantain, bit it, and chewed with a satisfied expression in place.

Shaz opened his mouth for a rebuttal, but Paula's sharp glare stopped him. For years, their father had wanted to involve them in the business. When it was clear neither Martin nor Shaz was interested, he continued building for the future, as he liked to say.

The way Dad was looking at him now, made Shaz uncomfortable. He loved his parents and valued every sacrifice they made to give him an education, but he was not prepared to give up what he did on a daily basis to run a construction company. He'd stated his case ages ago and didn't look forward to what he suspected his parents might demand of him if Martin didn't man up and take over Bostwick Construction.

CHAPTER 5

Vikkas tapped the glossy surface of the conference table and all the men fell silent. They moved straight into business, giving updates on agenda items and discussing their strategy for each area. Close to the end of the meeting, Vikkas' gaze fell on Shaz. "How are you progressing with the data and recording systems and documentation within The Castle?"

"Generally, I'm looking at everything in the administrative office, file storage area slash library. It's a labyrinth in terms of figuring out what cords lead where and how they all tie together. I suspect that's deliberate." He sipped from the glass of water. "Specifically, I'm looking at New Visions Center."

The other eight men at the table remained still, waiting for what Shaz would say next. At last week's meeting, he aired his concerns about the questionable practices at New Visions. Their mentor, Khalil Germaine, had intended to give childless couples a smooth adoption process. But some things had gone awry and others had gone completely rogue.

"The lease agreement for the adoption agency seems fine. The rent is being paid and the outfit seems legit." Shaz paused and looked at Grant, the director responsible for The Castle's real estate dealings. Then his gaze shifted to Dro, whose role covered "special" assignments. "Some of the adoptions are questionable, including one I'm dealing with now. And they all seem to link back to—"

"Alderman Darryl Bennett." Dro nodded slowly and drummed his fingers gently on the table.

"How'd you pick that up so fast?" Shaz asked, closing the file he'd been consulting.

"Lucky guess?" Dro grinned, then explained, "He's a director for the adoption center and his name has come up before in relation to your client."

Shaz tipped his head imperceptibly in thanks. He appreciated Dro not making his business with Camilla public, despite them being among brothers.

Grant eased away from the circular table and turned toward the building pictured on the screen at the back of the room. "D'you want to me look into their operations? I'm talking about business practices. Khalil does have a seat on the board of directors and thirty percent of the shares."

Nodding, Shaz said, "I'd appreciate it. As fast as you can get it done, but don't ruffle any feathers."

Grant cut him a hard look. "Trust that I know how to handle my business."

A faint smile crossed Shaz's lips. "My bad. I should know better, but on the other side of things, my client is giving me some anxious moments, trying to take things into her own hands."

"Apology accepted," Grant nodded and turned his attention to Vikkas, who pushed back from the table.

"If there are no other matters, can someone move for the termination of this meeting?"

Three hands went up and a moment later, the men gathered their documents and broke into groups as they filtered out of The Castle's boardroom.

Dro dropped into the seat next to Shaz. A low chuckle accompanied his words. "I sense there's trouble in Camillaland."

After closing the file in front of him, Shaz massaged his temples with one hand. "You could say that. I'm trying to keep her out of trouble. Last week, she stormed Bennett's office. This morning, she threatened to go to the newspapers with her story."

Dro's dimples showed up again. "Lady Camilla sounds like a full-time job."

"Tell me about it." Shaz got to his feet and picked up his portfolio. "I only convinced her to back down by saying I'd drop her case. Even then, she was giving me lip."

They exited the room and as they made it to the elevator, Shaz glanced sideways at Dro. "There's something I'll need you to do."

"Shoot." Dro's dark eyes focused on his.

Shaz waited until the elevator door closed, giving them privacy, before he spoke. "I want to have a talk with the father of Camilla's baby if possible, but before that, I need to know about his finances. Specifically, what made him so desperate he'd think it was okay to give up Camilla's baby without her knowledge."

"What is the timeline you're working with?"

Meeting his gaze, Shaz said, "The Bennetts had the paperwork drawn up two weeks ago."

Concern creased Dro's forehead. "So you're saying they're rushing this thing through?"

"With indecent haste."

While running a hand over the back of his head, Dro asked, "How is this even possible?"

Shrugging, Shaz said, "It's easy when the mother is running around arranging treatment and trying to straighten out her documents. By the way, are we making any headway on that situation?"

A muted ping indicated they were almost at their destination.

"I'm in touch with someone from DHS, but things are looking sticky." Dro shoved a hand through his hair, ruffling it. While smoothing the mess he made, he added, "With her passport and visa both expiring, Camilla must go back to Jamaica. The renewal of her passport is doable at the Jamaican consulate in Chicago. The U.S. visa renewal *must* be done from the island. There's no getting around it. And that's where this whole thing could fall apart."

The bottom dropped out of Shaz's stomach. "In this kind of

emergency, wouldn't some leniency apply?"

The elevator doors opened and they walked into the foyer. Only the red-haired concierge was in sight. With raised hands, Shaz and Dro acknowledged him as they strolled past the counter and waiting area that befitted a five-star hotel. When they stood in front of the building, Dro looked him square in the eyes. "Maybe five years ago, but with the government rounding up people and deporting them, I'm giving you the best option."

"Trust me, I understand. Better that than being herded into some facility and being shipped somewhere we'll never find her." He shuffled the files he carried to his left hand and held out the other to Dro. "Thanks, man."

Dro ignored his hand and pulled him in for a man hug. When they stood apart, he said, "Don't thank me yet because I've got more bad news." With a hand resting on Shaz's shoulder, he continued, "People—mostly kids—here for life-saving treatment have received deportation orders."

His body went cold, but Shaz shook his head. "Nah man, that's not even possible."

Dro didn't crack a smile. "You best believe it. That's the government's latest strategy to get rid of immigrants. I don't envy you the job of telling Camilla what I just told you."

A BMW pulled up at the entrance and a long-standing member of the Castle eased out of the vehicle. The businessman nodded at them and entered the building, now wired with Daron's surveillance equipment.

"That's heavy stuff for a mother to hear." Shaz tipped his head toward the sky, working the tension from the back of his neck. "In my line of work, I've delivered more bad news than most people have in a lifetime. Things could always be worse."

Frowning, Dro asked, "How so?"

"She has relatives here, so if she has to leave the baby for a short time—"

With a shake of the head, Dro stopped him. "Clearly, you have no small children in your family."

"Why d'you think that?" Shaz asked. "I have cousins on my mother's side of the family."

"If you were in touch, you'd know it would kill Camilla if she has to leave that baby with anybody. I don't care who it is."

Shaz ran the gold chain and medallion in his pocket through his fingers. The memento was a constant reminder of why he chose to work with immigrants. For years, his father had worn the chain as a reminder of the promise he'd made to their family. Shaz should have known better than to think that approach would work with Camilla. "I hear you, man. Talk later," he said.

They walked in silence to the parking lot, and when Shaz powered up the Alfa Romeo and sat inside, Camilla's lack of options hit him square in the chest. Before he drove away, his phone came to life. Camilla's numbers showed on the screen.

With a smile in his voice, he said, "I hope you haven't done anything I'll have to undo."

"Since I can't help Ayanna from a jail cell, I took your advice."

"That's good to know." A pleasing warmth spread in his chest as he asked, "So, what d'you need from me?"

A beep interrupted and he asked Camilla to hold on. The incoming call number wasn't familiar, but Shaz could make an accurate guess about the identity of the caller. He pulled in a deep breath and his lips twisted in a half smile as he said, "Shaz Bostwick. What can I do for you today?"

CHAPTER 6

The man across Shaz's desk had flat, pale-blue eyes.

Like they belong to a dead fish.

Peter Milholland's bald head carried a fringe of wispy brown hair and his pleasant smile hid a sharp, calculating mind. When he called earlier, Shaz promised him a half-hour slot at 5:00 p.m. rather than putting him off for another day. Only because of Camilla.

He didn't ask how the man came by his cell number. In his line of work, nothing surprised Shaz and people who needed to find him stopped at nothing to make contact.

Milholland laid a file on the edge of Shaz's mahogany desk and glanced at Darryl Bennett, seated next to him. "Thanks for seeing us at such short notice."

"You did say you had an urgent matter you needed to resolve today." The only reason Shaz agreed to fit in the Alderman and his lawyer was to find out how far along they were with the bogus adoption arranged by Ayanna's father. Shaz raised one hand, palm up, in a gesture for Milholland to state his case.

The man cleared his throat and tapped the file on the desk. "We urgently need to tie up my client's adoption, but we've encountered some hitches."

Elbows on the desk and fingers steepled below his chin, Shaz said, "Including the fact that the child in question is *not* up for adoption?"

Milholland lips pulled into a dry smile that didn't reach his eyes. "There must be a misunderstanding."

"I'm sure there is." Shaz sat back and moved his locs over one shoulder. "Another thing I'm sure of, is that you're here to give what you believe is a rational explanation."

"Yes, there is." The lawyer sat forward with an earnest expression in place. "Derrick Porter gave express permission for this to happen. In fact—"

Shaz shifted his attention to Bennett. "Apparently, your client forgot to inform you that I told him whatever deal he struck is off."

Pointing to the file, Milholland said, "These documents are perfectly legal—"

"They may very well be." Shaz rubbed his jaw, but kept his gaze locked on Milholland. "But can you explain to me how the mother of the child has no prior knowledge her daughter is about to be adopted?"

Bennett, who'd sat motionless, shuffled and exchanged a warning look with his lawyer.

"I'm certain that you're mistaken." A dull flush crept up from Milholland's collar and suffused his pasty face. He threw another glance sideways at his client before meeting Shaz's gaze. "Given the circumstances …"

Shaz didn't move, other than to pull in a breath. He was growing irritated with the verbal gymnastics. "Now would be a good time to explain these *circumstances*."

Milholland straightened his tie and cleared his throat. "The situation is, the child needs treatment for a heart condition and Porter doesn't have the resources to handle her care and the medical bills."

Nodding slowly as if in thought, Shaz met the man's eyes. "About the mother … ?"

Bennett leaned forward. "Porter said she was dead—"

"But you know she isn't." Shaz laid both hands on the desktop and lowered his voice. "So explain to me, how you plan to give her child to the alderman *without* her permission."

A beat of time went by before the lawyer hedged, "I'm sure there's a misunderstanding. We can get Porter and straighten—"

"No." Shaz's voice was like the crack of a whip between them. "What you're going to do is stand down. This adoption is illegal and if you persist—"

"What exactly are you going to do?" Bennett asked with a sneer, his eyes blazing. "How is she going to take care of her child when she's deported?"

His gaze strayed to the eggshell-blue wall behind Shaz. "It's in my power to protect Ayanna from deportation *if* she's in my care. Ms. Gibson is another matter."

Lasering the alderman with a glare, Shaz said, "So you know about *that*, huh? Seems you're filtering the information you give your lawyer."

Bennett dropped his gaze and heaved his shoulders. "It's not a secret that she's in a difficult situation."

"Any way you take it, as good as dead, eh?" A trace of humor colored Shaz's voice.

Milholland winced and cleared his throat a second time. "Now that we know she's alive, we can simply get her permission. The difficulty of her situation is sure to make her think about the best interest of the child."

"Don't let these locs fool you." Shaz glared at Milholland. "I'm not a country bumpkin on his first outing in the city. Nor do I smoke weed. One thing is sure, Camilla Gibson isn't going to agree to you taking her child simply because you struck a deal with the man who fathered that baby. A man who barely acknowledged he had a child and hasn't contributed much of anything to her welfare."

"Wouldn't it be simpler for her to agree to the adoption?" Bennett opened both hands in the air as though his proposal was perfectly logical. "With all the bills piling up …"

"That's not your business or mine." Shaz pushed back his sleeve to look at his watch, then neatened the papers on the desk. "Gentlemen. You've taken up more time than I have to give. I have another appointment elsewhere."

Milholland's skin flushed and his eyes glinted with frustration. "But what about our business? My client—"

"Your client would do better to find another baby to adopt." Shaz's gaze locked on Bennett. He stared at him long and hard before asking. "Why *this* particular child?"

A tic beat at one corner of Bennett's eye. He squared his shoulders and rested a finger over the spot. "My wife does volunteer work at the hospital. She met Ayanna there."

"Hmm. And I suppose she asked the relevant questions and you made the required moves."

Bennett pressed his fleshy lips together, then sighed, sounding wearier than he appeared. "We have no children and my wife—"

Shaz mulled that over. "Save it," he said, getting to his feet. "This baby is her mother's only child too. Since you kicked this off on the wrong foot, it shouldn't be too hard to start over with the right parents, speaking of which …" He gestured toward the door. "New Visions is too much of an exclusive outfit to be part of anything underhanded. If news should filter to the media …"

Bennett shot to his feet, scowling. "You wouldn't dare."

"I'm not one for making threats. I simply take action when it's required."

Milholland flapped both hands in the air as he stood. "Now, Mr. Bostwick, there's no need for that. I'm sure we can work this out like the gentlemen we are."

His cold eyes and false smile irked the hell out of Shaz, who wanted the two of them gone. "Don't tell me what I am or am not," he said, "This meeting is over."

Milholland's narrow nostrils widened and he pulled his head back and if he'd been slapped. "Now look here, young man …"

Hands shoved into his pockets, Shaz tipped his head toward him. "Yes?"

After a silent battle of wills during which nothing was achieved for the visitors, Milholland backed down. "We'll be in touch."

As both men went through the door, Shaz landed a parting blow. "I'm not sure why, but when you do, I hope it will be about another matter. Please close the door when you leave."

Bennett sent a vicious glare over his shoulder as waves of annoyance and something darker flowed off him.

This wasn't Shaz's first time around the block, so it would take a bit more than that to frighten him. He shook it off, but couldn't do anything about the unease that slithered through him, leaving goose bumps on his skin. His scalp also prickled, as if someone had walked over his grave.

CHAPTER 7

When the door closed, Shaz picked up the phone. While waiting to connect with one of the Kings, he drummed a staccato beat on the edge of the desk. One good thing his appointment to the board had done was to reconnect him with his brothers from the Macro International Magnet School.

The other was to bring him back under Khalil's influence. Shaz owed him much for changing the trajectory of his life. Teddy Bostwick had taught him about integrity and how to love and care for family, but Khalil had broadened his mind. He'd given him a list of required reading that changed the way he looked at life. Even now, he still had a couple of those eye-opening books in his possession, including Mahatma Gandhi's autobiography.

"Shaz, what can I do for you?"

"Everything good in tech land?"

"Never a dull moment." The calm, assured response was typical for the engineer-turned-security-consultant, Daron Kincaid.

"I asked you about New Visions today, but now I need information on a couple of men involved in the adoption agency. Names are Darryl Bennett and Peter Milholland."

"Are we talking FBI kind of details?"

"Everything you can find on these guys, including stuff that's under the radar."

Daron chuckled. "If I were a doctor, you'd be asking for a complete history."

One side of Shaz's mouth lifted in a grin. "Something like that."

"How soon? I sense that you need it a lot earlier than you indicated today."

"Fast track it." With his gaze on the laptop screen where he'd pulled up an adoption file that had red flags all over it, Shaz added, "I need this like yesterday."

With quiet assurance Daron said, "I'll be back with you by morning with everything."

"Thanks, Bro."

"You know it's all for one and one for all."

Shaz nodded at Daron's quip and made a sound of agreement. They'd all pledged that they would do everything to protect each other and Khalil Germaine since their appointment at The Castle a month ago. To a man, all nine of them were involved in turning over every stone to clean up The Castle and its operations. But their biggest assignment was unravelling the mystery of which members of the previous board were involved in the assassination attempt on Khalil.

The phone buzzed at Shaz's elbow, bringing his focus back to the office. He hit the hands-free button. "Yes, Elise."

"You need to leave." Her firm tone was the one she used when he'd committed to be elsewhere and shouldn't bury himself behind the desk.

"Thanks." He eyed the clock on his desk. "I'm on my way."

He closed the laptop, picked up his phone and iPad, then strode through the office. On his way out, he bade Elise goodbye.

"Remember you have an early meeting tomorrow," she lectured, as he walked by her station in one corner of the lobby.

He nodded and held up the iPad and smartphone. "As if I'd forget. Thanks all the same."

Her cheeky grin preceded a smart remark. "Whatever Boss Man. I'll call you at seven."

"Thanks, Elise."

The spunky woman—with skin the color of cocoa beans was as

thin as a rail and wore a neat afro—wasn't about to let him forget that whenever he went to the gym, he pushed hard and tended to get off to a slower start on the following morning.

As soon as he pulled out of the parking lot, he let Chris know he was en route to the center. Shaz could have used any of Evanston's gyms, but he believed in having the boys know there was nothing wrong with where they came from. Plus, they should support their community. Always.

Within fifteen minutes, Shaz was inside the locker room. Changed and ready to work out, he gathered the boys and split them into groups according to which muscles they were working on that day. The instructor he hired worked with the boys, giving them individual attention.

While wrapping his mind around the best angle to work Camilla's case from, Shaz concentrated on his abs routine. He had an impressive six pack but never slacked off on abs days. Shaz believed in honing his body, same as his mind. Khalil had impressed on the Kings the importance of balance.

No matter what you do in life, ensure body, mind, and spirit are in a harmonious relationship.

The session lasted an hour, after which the boys showered and got snacks while Shaz quizzed them on school and what was going on in their lives. Some of them spent each weekday afternoon on the property, which functioned as a homework center and a place where they were off the streets between the time they left school and when they were picked up, or when it was time to walk home.

Half the boys came from dysfunctional families. Others lived in single-parent homes, so the center provided some level of stability in their lives. Their outfit operated through a few volunteers, as well as paid staff who showed up in the afternoons and worked into the evenings.

"Everybody all right?" Shaz asked, on entering the rec room.

A rumble of voices agreed they were good.

"See you on Wednesday, all being well." He added that rider because the boys knew his schedule was unpredictable.

Another chorus rose in the room. "Bye, Shaz."

Shaz touched base with Chris, whose career path as an ex-basketball star and investor in the music industry allowed him to spend more time with the young men. With the assurance that Chris would be in-house on Wednesday, Shaz was free to leave.

Before he stepped out of the gym, he scanned the adjacent buildings. The wall of tinted windows at the front of the brick and glass structure allowed for privacy inside the club. Aside from the Alfa Romeo and Chris's Escalade, only a few other vehicles remained in the area.

Across the street, a guy sat slouched in the driver's seat of a black Toyota Camry. Frowning, Shaz recalled that he'd noticed the car while he was resting after a set of leg presses and it still hadn't moved. The vehicle wasn't familiar and very few of the boys' parents had rides.

When he realized Shaz had eyes on him, the man in the car sank lower in the seat. On a hunch, Shaz pushed the door open, taking slow, even steps until he stood next to the car.

"You're waiting for someone inside?" he asked, gesturing over his shoulder.

"Why you asking?" The man said, moving the toothpick in his mouth from one side to the other.

"Since you're answering my question with a question, I have a right to be suspicious." Arms folded, Shaz curled one corner of his mouth. "So, like I said, are you waiting for one of the boys?"

"No." The guy sat up and ran a hand over his beard. "You security or the police?"

"No, but I figure they'd be interested in someone loitering here for at least an hour."

Panic flashed in the man's eyes, but he blustered, "The last time I checked, this was a free country."

"Well, I'm here to tell you that in this zone, we view any loiterers with suspicion." Eyes narrowed, Shaz folded his arms. "Unless you're here for a specific reason."

Something shifted in the guy's eyes. "Like I said, this is a free country."

His skin prickled, just as it had earlier in the meeting when Bennett left the office. Shaz figured he'd hit the nail on the head. The harder he looked, the more familiar the young man seemed to him, but his mind couldn't grasp how he knew him.

Shaz leaned toward the car. "Here's a message for whoever sent you. I don't scare easy."

That said, he switched on the engine of the SUV, walked to the front of the Camry, and crossed the street. While he memorized the licence plate number, he allowed the Marley CD to spool to Buffalo Soldier and pulled away from the sidewalk. The music soothed him and he undid his locs, throwing the thin leather band on the seat next to him.

When he got to the end of the street, he checked the mirror. The black Camry had pulled onto the road and was several feet behind him. Instead of turning toward the place he used to call home, at the North East end of Evanston, Shaz headed downtown. He was at the intersection when he shot another glance at the mirror, then squinted. The Toyota was several vehicles behind. He didn't get why the man would be so bold.

Shaz went across the next block and circled back, heading downtown. As he did, he dialed Dro, engaging the hands-free system. "Is it possible to check on a licence plate number and let me know where it leads?"

"Is there pepper in jerked chicken?" Dro asked with a chuckle. "And by the way, are you in trouble?"

Shaz's attention went to the car still in his range of vision. He sped up, wanting to disprove the theory that the idiot was following him. "No. Not yet."

"Well, apply the brakes." Dro chuckled. "I'll have this information for you before you get there."

"Thanks, man," Shaz said, as the driver of the Camry attempted to overtake the vehicle ahead of him. Shaz grunted as he spun the wheel and the car behind him kept pace. He maneuvered between two cars, causing the driver behind him to honk at length and mash his brakes.

"Shaz?"

The muted sound of metal grinding together drew Shaz's eyes back to the rearview mirror. His stalker had rear ended the car ahead of him.

A smile came to Shaz's lips and he answered Dro as he sped away. "I'm here, man."

"Be careful."

"Sure." With one last look at the traffic snarl behind him, Shaz smirked. He wasn't sure whether the guy following him was connected to the alderman, but he wouldn't be surprised if that was the case. They'd learn he was no pretty boy without the skills to handle himself.

CHAPTER 8

Camilla placed a gentle kiss on Ayanna's head. The soft, fuzzy hair tickled her nose, reminding her of Derrick. He also had downy hair, thanks to his grandmother who had East Indian ancestors. She'd learned too late that was the softest part of him, because the man had no heart. His actions in the past couple of months proved her relationship with him had been a mistake from the get-go.

"Mommy." Ayanna giggled and rested the back of her head against Camilla's chest.

"What d'you need, Boo?" She pressed another kiss to Ayanna's hair as her thoughts spun back to Derrick.

A blazing-hot attraction and whirlwind romance during a five-month stint when she was in Chicago three years ago meant little time to find out the nitty-gritty details. She left good sense behind when she fell for his good looks and charisma. By the time she found out she was pregnant, she'd already broken things off with him. Ayanna was the one link they shared. Yet, Derrick was trying to rip away the most precious gift he'd given Camilla.

The nerve of him to want to *visit* when he was trying to offload their child to other people. Even now, she couldn't see behind it, but for the fact that she knew about his love of gambling, the financial hole he might be in, and the lengths he'd go to pay his debts.

If he hadn't left when he did the other night, the police might have eventually charged her with assault. During their heated argument—in which Aunt Mabel had to intervene—Camilla thought they would have come to blows, but Derrick backed down and left without seeing Ayanna.

Long after his tires screeched at the end of the street, Camilla stood behind the door hyperventilating, certain he'd find a way to come back and snatch Ayanna.

Her gaze landed on Shaz, standing across his parents' yard talking to his father and brothers, wearing a black cable knit sweater and jeans. The man was sexy with a capital S-E-X-Y, but wasn't that what had led her into trouble with Derrick?

She'd been pleasantly surprised, and a bit apprehensive, when Mrs. Bostwick called her a day and a half ago and invited her to a barbeque at their house on Friday evening. She could only have gotten her number from Shaz or Aunt Mabel. At first, Camilla thought Mrs. Bostwick wanted to interrogate her face to face about the relationship between her and Shaz, but that didn't seem to be the case. Or, she hadn't gotten around to what she wanted to find out as yet.

Paula Bostwick had chit-chatted with her on the phone for five minutes, before issuing the invitation with such warmth that Camilla couldn't decline without seeming ungrateful.

"He's handsome, isn't he?" Mrs. Bostwick said, claiming the seat next to Camilla on a patio chair under the shade of an elm. "And my favorite, too."

Somehow, Camilla didn't buy that. Mrs. Bostwick struck her as a wise woman, who knew how to handle her family with deftness and grace.

"I'm sure you haven't told him that in front of the others." When Camilla looked sideways at Mrs. Bostwick, she gave her a conspiratorial wink.

"He's the best looking of the lot though."

Camilla's lips twitched, then she said, "Would you consider me biased if I said yes?"

A throaty laugh was her response. "You're a smart one."

"And so are you," Camilla said, as her attention went back to Shaz, "because I'm sure you've told all your children they're your favorite."

Again, Mrs. Bostwick laughed. This time, she admitted nothing. "Mabel told me all about you."

A tad discomfited, Camilla let her gaze slide to the small, serene woman who clearly ruled the men in her family gently, yet firmly. She sensed Paula Bostwick could be a formidable enemy.

Thankfully, she seemed friendly enough and didn't give off any weird vibes. Her aura was the same as when they met at Aunt Mabel's church some weeks ago.

The men's laughter floated to them on the wind and Camilla couldn't resist stealing another look at Shaz.

"I hope she didn't share all my dark secrets," Camilla teased, holding Ayanna at the waist as she shook a brown-skinned rag doll by the legs.

Paula Bostwick chuckled. "You know Mabel well. Actually, she gave me a synopsis of your situation after she introduced us." Mrs. Bostwick's focus went to Shaz, then returned to Camilla. "Shastra filled in the details of how you met and what an impact you've had on him."

She settled further back into the seat, folding both hands in her lap. Her aqua shirt was an identical match to her husband's Polo. They both also wore jeans. Paula's eyes drifted toward her son again. "Or course, I had to meet the woman Shastra actually felt comfortable talking about with me. Perhaps because he knows Mabel and I are friends and serve in the same ministries at church."

Camilla swiped her lips with the tip of her tongue. What exactly had they told Shaz's mother?

"Don't worry," she said, patting Camilla's arm. "My son is a great judge of character. If you're okay with him, then you're all right with me."

"Thank you," Camilla said, lifting Ayanna and repositioning her. "I appreciate you welcoming me, despite everything."

Paula Bostwick met her eyes. "To be frank, I wanted to feel you out for myself." As she smiled, she admitted, "I like what I've seen and heard so far."

"Mrs. Bostwick, I—"

"Call me Aunt Paula," she said, glancing at the four men across the yard again.

Camilla dipped her head to acknowledge the comment. "Thanks. I was wondering why I'm the only one here outside of your sons and Denise, who suddenly disappeared."

She had wondered why the younger woman went missing without any explanation.

"You're also observant." Paula's smile widened. "If you can hold your own in this family, then it tells me something about you." Tipping her chin toward the men, she added, "They're my world and if you get along with them …" Laughing, and blowing a kiss at Ayanna, she added, "And by the way, now that we've eaten, Denise is probably inside talking on the phone."

"Now that you mention it, dinner was delicious." Camilla lowered Ayanna to the ground, then continued, "I've never had jerked pork that tender. I even enjoyed the crackling."

She'd snagged a bit of the crispy pork skin off Shaz's plate, laughing when he frowned over losing the morsel he'd been saving to eat last. He gave her the stink eye and his family teased him about his inability to give up food, even for that special someone.

"Teddy and I are now a tag team and have cooking down to a fine art. Comes from when I started teaching and he'd season the meat in the mornings and I'd come home and do the cooking after school while he was at the construction site."

"How long have you been married?" Camilla asked, spreading the crinkled material of her dress over her legs.

Wearing a proud smile, Paula said, "Forty-two years."

"Wow. My parents would have celebrated thirty-five years, if my father was still alive."

When Aunt Paula tipped one eyebrow, Camilla added. "He died in a car accident when I was twenty. That was ten years ago."

The sudden pain took Camilla by surprise because it had been a while since she allowed herself to dwell on his passing. He'd had such a profound impact during her formative years, she'd hoped that Ayanna would have the same kind of relationship with Derrick despite their differences. So much for that.

Aunt Paula patted her hand. "I know losing a parent is hard, but—"

The men's raised voices distracted Aunt Paula, who frowned and got to her feet. "Excuse me," she said, as Shaz stalked toward them.

Aunt Paula met him halfway across the grass. "Shastra?"

Although she didn't hear what Shaz said to his mother, his features gave away his mood. Both brows pulled together in dark slashes that revealed the depth of his irritation. His flared nostrils also betrayed his feelings.

His father and brothers still stood together, and Roman gesticulated toward Shaz and shook his head. Martin rocked on the balls of his feet while he stared at the grass. Mr. Bostwick folded his arms and shook his head, but his scowl was hard to miss.

When Camilla's attention settled on Shaz, he asked, "You ready?"

"I guess I have to be if you are."

His mouth curved in a pseudo-smile as he picked up Ayanna. "How about you, princess?"

Ayanna's usual incoherent response amused Shaz, which in turn lessened Camilla's concern. "Let me tell everyone thanks, then we can go."

She spent the next few minutes talking with his family as the heat of the sun waned and the evening grew cooler. She exchanged hugs with Aunt Paula and Denise, and noticed Martin's indifference before strapping Ayana into the car seat and sitting beside Shaz in the Alfa Romeo.

The ride home took twenty minutes, during which Shaz said next to nothing. In front of Aunt Mabel's house, Camilla unsnapped the seat belt and sat sideways. "Mind telling me who stole your binky."

Shaz cut his eyes at her. "That's not even funny."

She shrugged, trying not to laugh. "First you were in a good mood. Then, you were not. With no stops in between. What happened to turn things around so fast?"

With one hand, Shaz scratched his hair, which had been freshly groomed. "It's my family."

"Well, that's fairly obvious and I don't need to be a top-notch lawyer to argue that case." She smiled when she glanced at Ayanna, who had fallen asleep.

Shaz threw Camilla another bad look, which only made her giggle. Squeezing his rock-hard bicep, she teased, "Come on, whatever it is can't be that bad. Good thing Ayanna's sleeping. You'd frighten her with that face."

He studied her for a couple of seconds, then sighed. "You're right. I shouldn't allow others to spoil my day."

After glancing at the house, where the absence of flickering shadows told the tale that Aunt Mabel wasn't sitting in her regular spot in front of the television, Camilla said. "Auntie isn't home yet, if you want to come inside and tell me what has you vexed like this …"

He didn't agree or disagree, so Camilla handed him the key to the front door, opened the vehicle, and went to release Ayanna from the seat. By the time she cradled Ayanna in her arms, Shaz stood behind her. "Hey, I could have helped."

"It's okay." She squashed a smile at his grinch-like expression. "Please bring the seat."

He turned on his heels and did as she asked.

Once they stepped into the house, she laid Ayanna in her playpen and came back to find Shaz prowling the living room with the phone pressed to his ear. She curled on the large sofa and watched him as his complexion darkened to a ruddy shade.

"I didn't 'cut', as you put it, because I'm selfish," he said, and Camilla knew he was still uptight from the way his skin flushed. "I left because you all were annoying the shit out of me. When did I get to be first in line to assume control of the business? The two of you know I'm not interested. I love what I do and I'm not giving up my work to run the company."

He listened while doing more damage to his neat hair, which she badly wanted to smooth. "Dad knows I've never been interested. Martin is the sensible choice. He's already in that line of business, just as you. He's just stubborn. I wish you all would—"

Shaz sat next to her, rubbing his forehead. "Bottom line? My answer is still no."

A tic danced beside his eye, and Camilla placed a finger on the spot. He froze, accepted her subtle message, and let out his breath. "I have to go now, and just so you know, this subject is closed."

His movement was controlled when he laid the phone on the center table. He blew out a long, slow breath, then ran both hands over his hair. "I guess you now understand what was eating me."

Camilla rubbed his back, but didn't speak.

"The long and short of it is that Roman and my father want me to run the family business." A long pause punctuated the conversation before he added, "I'm not about to change my career for anyone. Not even family."

Nodding slowly, Camilla said, "I understand. You're good at what you do. Everybody says you're the best."

"Now if only *you'd* believe it." A wry smile lifted his mouth.

"Oh, I believe in you. In such a way that I can't help wishing I'd met you before I made the biggest mistake of my life." She couldn't help her bitter tone when she spat, "Derrick."

Meeting Shaz's gaze, she whispered, "Don't get me wrong, Ayanna is the best thing that came out of that disaster."

Shaz cupped her jaw and stroked her skin with the pad of his thumb. "Don't get stuck in regrets. The future is ahead of you. The past only has the power to harm you if you let it."

"I know," she whispered.

His touch on her skin was hypnotic and soothing. "That's why we should make the present count, despite the challenges."

With all the threats coming at her, plus the unexpected turns with Ayanna's health, she'd be lying if she said she didn't do more than her fair share of worrying. Derrick was another major source of concern. She'd heard whispers through social media that there was little he wouldn't do to feed his addiction to gambling. His treatment of Ayanna made her think there was truth to that rumor. Like they said in Jamaica, *If it don't go so, it nearly go so,* which meant that while a piece of news might not be a hundred percent accurate, it still had elements of truth to it.

"You worry too much," Shaz murmured. "I see it in your eyes."

His lips brushed hers, then settled, urging her to let him inside. As her mouth opened under his expert touch, Camilla's thoughts stopped churning and she let Shaz kiss away her fears.

CHAPTER 9

Before his gaze returned to Camilla, Shaz did a visual sweep of their surroundings. They'd had lunch and he took them to the park to walk off the food and give Ayanna a treat at the same time.

Camilla's intense concentration on her daughter fascinated him and he could barely pull his eyes away from them.

While Ayanna pointed toward the shore, she let loose a string of garbled words, then yelled, "Mommy, dog."

"Yes, baby." Camilla's smile was captivating. Her eyes sparkled and the joy in them stole his breath.

Shaz wanted every bit of that directed at him. He scanned the area around them again, conscious that the park bench left them wide open to anyone who meant them harm. Over the past few days, he had the uncomfortable feeling he was being watched. He hadn't seen anything out of the ordinary, but the sixth sense his grandmother told him would serve him well in life, kept him on edge. Plus, he was conscious of his run-in with that thug a few days ago. By now, the man's car would probably be in repair but that didn't mean he'd given up on shadowing him.

They sat under a tree on a park bench with the baby bag between them. Groups of people moved in both directions, cycling, skating, and strolling.

When his gaze went back to Camilla, he took her hand. "Have you changed your mind about going home?"

She shook her head. "I'm not leaving her here."

"Don't you have family you trust?"

Looking sideways at him, she said, "I trust Auntie Mabel, but she has the restaurant."

"What about your other people?"

"They work." Her tone was clipped and warned him not to press. "You know why I don't trust anybody. Not after what Derrick did."

A skateboarder zipped past, distracting Shaz. When he looked back at her, he said, "I truly understand that, but d'you hear what's going on in the news?"

Her eyebrow arched, encouraging him to continue.

Over Ayanna's babbling, he said, "Illegal immigrants. The way they're treated." He let his words sink in. "D'you want to find yourself in that situation?"

Ayanna squealed and pointed at a black and brown Terrier, who trotted by on a leash. After kissing the little girl's cheek, Camilla met his eyes. "That's not likely to happen to me. I'm not trying to stay here permanently."

Her words caused a pang in the region of his heart. Shaz ignored it and pressed on. "You can't be here on an expired visa. You will be deported. Unless …"

She shook her head. "I have better sense than that. Jamaica is my home."

"I understand that." He stared at his shoes, then swallowed a sigh. "Negotiating is easier when you have a leg to stand on."

"Are you chastising me?" she asked, pulling a coil of her hair out of Ayanna's tiny fist. The breeze ruffled the rest of it, shrouding her face in layered waves that flattered her face.

Shaz chuckled. "Take it however you like. I'm thinking about what's best for you and Ayanna."

"I know." She squeezed his fingers while holding Ayanna around the waist with her other hand. "Thanks for picking us up from the hospital."

For a few seconds, she closed her eyes. She hadn't complained, but he felt the stress coming off her in waves when he met her in front of the facility. In reply to her question of what he was doing there, he explained that he'd gone to Aunt Mabel's and she directed him to the hospital. He dared not tell Camilla her aunt commanded him to pick her up.

"Not a problem."

Ayanna sat, pulling at the neckline of Camilla's loose blouse, exposing the royal blue tank top that hugged her breasts. He shut down his immediate thoughts and cleared his throat, happy that the breeze kept Camilla busy, pushing the hair away from her face.

"After Ayanna has her procedure, it may be good to have her visit the holistic center at The Castle. Jai Maharaj, a friend of mine, will have it up and running by then. His approach to treatment is less invasive. I'm sure that even after surgery, she can benefit from visiting."

"That's a thought," Camilla said, removing Ayanna's fingers from her mouth.

Camilla's changing micro-expressions and her casual response intrigued him. If he read them correctly, she was wondering how she'd pay for any service inside that exclusive property. Now wasn't the time to tell her he'd take care of it. The woman was not only independent, but feisty and wouldn't accept what Jamaicans called 'freeness' from him.

He turned his face up to the sun. The warmth of it was welcome. Although it was Saturday, he'd gone to the office today to deal with paperwork for his pro bono clients. His mind circled back to Camilla and her aunt and what they wouldn't allow him to do for them, without charging. Despite what Camilla told him about her sponsored travels for her blog and her work as a model, billing them didn't sit well with him. The last time he raised the argument, Camilla point blank told him she wouldn't accept that kind of help from a man with whom she wasn't intimately involved. Getting her to that point was high on his list of priorities, but they weren't there yet.

"You okay, Shaz?" Camilla asked, disrupting his thoughts.

"Yeah, I'm good." He shifted sideways and looked her in the eyes. "Actually, I'm not. I want you to level with me."

Her tone hinted at defensiveness when she asked, "In terms of what?"

"You. Ayanna. Porter."

He saw, rather than heard, her sigh. Apparently, she thought he was about to confront her about something else, but what?

"What d'you want to know?" Camilla asked.

"How did things get to the point where he'd think it's okay to give your child up for adoption?"

Camilla stared at the water drifting in the pond a few feet away and spoke in a monotone. "Derrick and I want different things."

"That's fairly obvious," he quipped.

A faint smile crossed her lips. Then she winced as Ayanna pulled her hair. "We met three years ago when I was here on vacation. We hit it off, but honestly we didn't spend enough time together. Long story short, I got pregnant. I wanted the baby. He didn't."

"Hmmm." Shaz scanned the area behind them that ran parallel to the road. "So, if he's not interested in being a father, why …"

"Derrick likes the slot machines and the races," Camilla said with a sour note in her voice.

"Are you saying there's actually a reason behind him trying to sell his baby?"

She winced, took a deep breath and stared over Ayanna's head. When she looked at him again, she spoke in a monotone. "You see, Derrick is from a dysfunctional family and when you're not grounded, you do crazy things."

In two minutes, she gave him a deeper understanding of the man she'd gotten involved with. Single working mother. Six kids raising each other. Not enough parental supervision. A taste for the fast life.

Her explanation backed up Daron's findings in the report he'd sent to Shaz. The added challenge of financial troubles sometimes made men desperate. But to sell his own flesh and blood was unthinkable.

The back of his neck prickled and he sat up. Casually, he got to his feet and stretched, looking around them. "We should go."

Camilla turned her face to the sun and sighed, while Ayanna grabbed her chin. "This break was good for us. Thank you."

"Not a problem." He picked up the baby bag and waited as she settled Ayanna in her arms. The little girl seemed worn out by the sights and sounds and was half asleep.

They chatted as they walked toward the SUV, but Shaz couldn't shake the unease in his gut. He put a hand to Camilla's back as he scanned the parking lot. From a few feet away, he opened the SUV remotely and deliberately slowed his steps, not wanting to alarm Camilla over what might be an overinflated sense of danger. Maybe his jumpiness had to do with Khalil's situation, which they were still unraveling at the Castle.

He held the back door behind the driver's seat open for Camilla to put Ayanna in the booster seat. A car door slammed and the scuffling of feet came from behind them. "Yo, Shaz."

At the sound of his name, he spun. Eyes narrowed, he took in the two men crowding him. *Small time thugs.*

He stepped in front of Camilla, who froze in the middle of strapping down Ayanna.

"Am I supposed to know you?" Shaz asked.

The man, who wore a do-rag and had a mouthful of gold grillwork, raised his hand as if to shake Shaz's. In his fist, he carried a small taser. His companion moved as if to get around Shz.

With both hands, Shaz shoved him in the chest. He staggered backward and fell to the asphalt.

His partner lunged toward Camilla, who ducked. The man pushed her to the side and yanked Ayanna out of the seat. He clutched her to his chest and turned took off running. The man on the ground scrambled to his feet and ran behind him.

Ayanna woke, screaming as the two men jumped into a black Camaro parked a couple of cars down the row.

Going on instinct, Shaz dived into the SUV, yelling as he sat. "Hop in, Cam."

Camilla had left his side, running toward the car that peeled out of its spot.

Curious onlookers stared with their jaws slack.

Seconds later, Shaz came abreast of Camilla, who screamed at the car with tears running down her cheeks.

"Get in," he yelled.

To her credit, Camilla responded immediately, running around the hood and jumping in beside him. "They took my baby. They took my baby."

The words came in an unbroken loop while she stared ahead, keeping the car in her line of sight.

Shaz squeezed her cold hand. "I know. I'm sorry. Hang on. We'll get her back."

He stepped on the gas, engaging the audio system and throwing a glance at Camilla as she buckled the seatbelt with trembling fingers. She braced both hands on the dashboard as he raced onto the road. Her lips moved as if she was praying and she dashed her knuckles over her cheeks.

Eyes trained on the car in front of them, Shaz gave the audio system a command. "Call Daron."

"The police," Camilla cried. "We need the police."

Shaz swung in and out of the sparse traffic, gaining on the Camaro.

When Daron picked up, Shaz said, "We have a situation."

In a few clipped sentences, he explained what happened.

"Don't hang up," Daron said. "I have people in the area."

Shaz overtook a car driven by a white-haired lady, who shook her fist at them when he came close to clipping the bumper. He swung around the red and black Smart car in front of them, barely avoiding collision with a Ford truck. The Camaro raced around a corner with Shaz directly behind. As he gained on the car, he threw caution aside and clipped the back of the Camaro.

The men kept going.

Camilla grabbed the dashboard, with her eyes trained on their target. "Come on," she muttered.

Daron came back on the line. "Where are you now?"

"Coming up to Sheridan Road."

"Bryson and Linc will be waiting."

"Thanks, man. Talk to you in a bit." Shaz ended the connection and rear-ended the car again.

The man in the back seat turned terrified eyes on them.

A smile that felt more like a grimace came to Shaz's face. He was attracting attention, but he was at the point of no return. "Hold on tight, Camilla."

She nodded, but didn't answer as she brushed at another tear.

He swung the SUV sideways and drew alongside the Camaro. The driver of the oncoming car blasted his horn and swung out of Shaz's way at the last moment. Spinning the wheel toward the Camaro, Shaz forced it sideways. The driver turned bulging eyes on him. When his attention shifted back to the road, he screamed.

CHAPTER 10

"Are you sure you're okay?" Camilla asked over her shoulder as she let them into Aunt Mabel's living room.

Wearing a wry smile, Shaz placed the car seat on the floor and sat next to Camilla on the sofa. "I should be asking you that."

He had insisted on taking them to Jaidev Maharaj to be sure Ayanna was okay. That took them over an hour and he didn't tell Camilla that detour was also an evasive move in case they picked up another tail that Daron's men weren't aware of.

After kissing Ayanna's cheek, Camilla turned her gaze on him. "As long as she's okay, I'm good. Let me put her down and I'll be with you in a minute."

When Camilla returned, she asked if he needed anything to drink.

Shaz shook his head. "I'm fine, and really happy we got Ayanna back."

Her gaze probed him as she responded to his comment. "After what you did back there, I'm not so sure I'll ever feel safe riding with you."

He folded both arms across his chest, surprised she hadn't taken him to task before this. "Did you want your baby back or not?"

She laid a hand on his wrist, then drew closer. "Don't get upset. I was teasing."

He waited, because he knew there was something else.

"Sorta." She looked at him as if she needed more of an explanation.

She wouldn't be getting one.

"You can thank my dad for teaching me defensive driving," he said. "And anyway, I did what I had to do in the moment."

Camilla attempted to speak, but Shaz interrupted her. "Speaking of which, d'you know any of those men?"

She answered immediately, but something flickered in her eyes. "Of course not."

"Are you sure?" Their gazes locked and he watched her keenly, allowing his instinct to lead him. Did she know something she wasn't saying?

"Yes, but …" She paused, staring at the blank television screen across the room. "What if Derrick set that up?"

"Then he'd be looking for more trouble." He gripped her arms and made her face him. "Let the authorities do their job."

"What authority?" Her brows winged upward and she all but rolled her eyes. "Those men who came looked more like private security to me."

"Don't worry about it." Shaz assumed a more neutral expression, hoping she didn't ask any more questions about Daron's crew. "They won't bother you again," he added.

"Spoken like someone who has clout to shift things about and make stuff happen." She folded her arms and narrowed a steely gaze on him. "So about that lamp post they ran into. Who's going to report that *accident*? And don't think I didn't notice how your people hustled the men into the back of their Jeep. I hope they don't turn up with broken bones or anything like that."

Or dead, was the unspoken sentiment.

Her frown deepened. "I trust you're not involved in anything Miss Paula wouldn't approve of. Auntie would have my head if you did any funny business on my behalf. She thinks the world of you."

"Trust me, I wouldn't want to get on the wrong side of those two women." As they laughed, Shaz made a mental note not to underestimate Camilla, who was more observant than he first thought.

Daron's three-man crew swept on the scene and carted the two would-be kidnappers away. Despite the group of onlookers, the third man backed up the Camaro and followed the Jeep. Shaz wondered what they'd have done if the car had been incapacitated. Plus, he'd been wondering if there were any street cameras to complicate things, but he doubted it. In any case, it was too late now to perplex his brain about things he couldn't fix. Knowing Daron and his technical toys, if there were cameras, he'd find a way to jam them or erase the footage. When his mind strayed to possible consequences of hacking into the city's computer system, Shaz shut down his thoughts.

With one arm around Camilla, he whispered, "I'll do everything in my power to protect you and Ayanna."

"I know." Camilla's eyes softened and she cupped his cheek. "Thank you."

Shaz turned his head and kissed her palm. "It's what any man would do."

"Don't be too sure about that." She hunched and hugged herself. "Tell you the truth, I'm a little scared. Why would anybody want to kidnap Ayanna?"

"Would Porter stoop to that?"

She hesitated. "Hard to tell, but if he has an agreement with that disgusting politician and money is his goal."

Despite his instinct and the text update Daron sent, Shaz allowed his mouth to say the opposite of what he suspected, though the park had been filled with other children. "Maybe it was a random occurrence."

With both hands, she combed through her hair and rested her elbows on both knees. "I sure hope so. It's bad enough that she's not well, but to think about her being a target." She sat up and peered at him. "D'you think Alderman Bennett could have anything to do with this?"

"He has no reason to do something that puts him at risk. Already, he's walking a fine line." He squeezed her to his side. "Sweets, don't get your brain in a knot over this. Are you willing to let me handle this in the way I see fit?"

After staring at him long and hard, she nodded.

"Good." He removed his arm as he went into planning mode. "I'm going to have someone watch you for the next week or so—"

"Wait a minute." She raised both hands. "Are you talking about security?"

"Yes, just until we're sure this was not deliberately aimed at you and Ayanna."

"I don't know, Shaz." Her frown conveyed her doubt and concern. "Already you're doing more than necessary for me. I don't want to be more indebted to you than I already am."

He pulled back a little. "More than necessary? We're further along in our relationship than you thinking I'm doing this as a favour to your auntie. Woman, I … let's just say what we share is more than a passing attraction."

Looking at her hands, she said, "I know, but I still don't understand how you can check for me like that when I've done some really stupid things. Like this whole situation."

"Cut yourself some slack, Cam. You were travelling and trying to raise the money you need for the surgery. Passport and visa issues crop up all the time. What we're dealing with here, is a bit more." He took her hand in his. "Let me do what I do best, and you worry about taking care of Ayanna, okay?"

Camilla pulled her hand from his and stroked the side of his face as her gaze went to his mouth. "Thank you," she whispered.

She leaned in until her lips brushed his. Then, her eyelids closed and her lips parted. With soft kisses, he eased her mouth open. A soft moan welcomed him as their tongues collided in a languorous dance that had Shaz gripping the back of her head with one hand.

Her fingers stroked his locs as he delved deeper and took control of the kiss. With more urgency, she clung to his neck letting out soft groans that told him they were in danger of crossing a line. He pulled back, pecking her lips, and fighting not to make physical contact with her again.

When she opened her eyes, they were hazy with need.

Unable to resist, he kissed her once more. He had a fever in his blood that he'd been holding back because of the business end of things, but each time he touched her, he was in danger of taking Camilla where he was sure she wasn't ready to go.

"Woman, you are dangerous," he said, kissing the corner of her mouth.

A sultry smile crept across her lips. "You think?"

"The only thing keeping me from taking you right here is the fact that Miss Mabel might walk in and kill the two of us for breaking her sofa."

His comment made Camilla laugh. "I have to check on Ayanna," she said as she got to her feet.

After watching the sway of her hips as she walked away, he sent a text to Daron to ask what information he'd gotten from the men. He responded within a couple of seconds.

Daron: Will send some details your way later. Give me more time.

Shaz: Can you put some security on Cam and the baby?

Daron: Not a problem. Send me the address. I'll deal with it now.

Shaz typed in the address and by the time Camilla walked back into the room, he was more at peace with leaving her.

"Baby okay?"

She nodded and sat facing him with one leg curled underneath her. "I thought about what you said. I may leave for a few days just to try and sort out the visa. I'm trying to make an emergency appointment with the Kingston embassy."

The concern and uncertainty etched on her face tugged at his heart. "Are you leaving her here?"

Camilla's eyes opened as if he insulted her. "Of course not."

"But—" He reached for her arm, but she shrank back.

She straightened in the seat. "I am *not* leaving Ayanna here."

"You can trust Aunt Mabel."

"I know that. It's Derrick and his family I have doubts about."

"So, isn't it possible—?"

"Shaz, that's a no." Her tone said the argument was finished.

"I was going to suggest—"

"The answer is no."

His phone pinged and he looked at the screen and let out his breath. He could leave.

Camilla's tense face almost deterred him from taking her hand again, but he rose and pulled her into an embrace. "I know you don't want to hear a word about separation from your baby, so I won't pursue that argument. What I will say is that no matter the situation, there are options."

When she attempted to speak, he laid a finger over her lips. "When the times comes and if you need those options, I will be here. For now, I have to go."

He touched his lips to hers and they walked toward the door. On the other side, the evening was growing cooler and dusk would fall in another hour.

A few yards up the street on the opposite side a dark-blue Jetta was parked. From the edge of the veranda he watched as the window was lowered. The person inside saluted Shaz, who returned the gesture.

"That's your man?" Camilla asked.

"Not exactly, but he'll make sure you're safe."

Arms folded, she looked up at him. "You suspect there's more to this than what we're seeing."

Her words were a statement rather than a question, so he chose not to answer. Instead, he moved in close and kissed her forehead. The less she suspected, the better it would be.

When he stepped back, he said, "I'm sure you'll tell Aunt Mabel what happened today, but I'd prefer if you don't tell her I have someone watching you."

Her smile was unexpected. "If she finds out, I'm telling her it was your idea."

"That's all right. I can deal with her." He pressed his lips to hers, then turned her toward the door. "Go inside and lock up."

"Talk to you tomorrow, Mr. Criminal Minds."

He chuckled, then moseyed down the steps and through the gate. Instead of going to the SUV, he walked across the street.

CHAPTER 11

Shaz needed a shower. His interaction with Milholland made him feel as if he'd been handling a snake and had wrapped it around him. He was getting the same reaction from the girl sitting in one of the visitor's chairs across from him. This was the second time she and her mother had come in to see him. Georgiana was afraid of her shadow and cowered if he made any sudden moves. In the time they'd been inside the office, Shaz had to suppress his anger and act as if his insides weren't at boiling point.

"Georgiana," he said, placing both elbows on his desk. "I can't help you if you won't tell me what I need to know."

Her lips trembled and she scratched her box braids as if confused. Her hands shook as she exchanged a fearful glance with her mother, who rubbed her arm from the Queen Anne chair she occupied. "You can trust him, Georgiana, since you don't want to go to the police about any of this."

Shaz understood that because of her reputation in her neighborhood, Georgiana didn't think the police would do anything about the threat she was facing.

"Was it something that happened here?" Shaz asked, his brows furrowed. "Someone you saw before you came in?"

Georgiana exchanged a petrified look with her mother and wrapped herself in a hug. The girl was tall and slender with a creamy complexion.

She'd be a real beauty when she grew into womanhood. Now, she was a terrified child who needed his help.

Shaz squinted as he allowed his mind to run. Georgiana had been just as timid the last time he saw her, but she also had a spark in her eyes as if she'd been feisty before her ordeal dampened her spirit. Today, when she walked in, she'd been in a state, clutching her mother and refusing to let go. From what he understood, her pimp had 'sold' her into a high-class house of prostitution.

His gaze went to the clock set in a golf ball on one side of his desk. Their half-hour session was almost over and they had made little to no progress.

He studied Georgiana's mother, who was a pretty woman in her early forties. With five children to feed, she had a careworn expression he'd seen all too often on his pro-bono clients. As his gaze shifted from mother to daughter and back, a lightbulb exploded in his head. "Was it Milholland?"

Eyes wide, the two females stared at him, as if they didn't have a clue what he meant.

He pointed toward the door. "The man you passed coming in. D'you know him?"

The girl's eyes filled with tears. She sprang to her feet and dashed out of the office.

"Georgiana!" Her mother hopped up and chased her through the door.

They were at the front entrance when Shaz caught up with them. Putting aside his anxiety to get to the root of what had the teenager scared out of her mind, he guided her back to reception and into one of the seats. In a silent exchange, he asked her mother to trust him. She nodded in acquiescence.

Thankfully, it was at the end of the day, so the waiting room was empty. With a tip of his head in her direction, he asked Elise to make herself scare.

She obeyed immediately and disappeared into the small office behind her desk.

 J. L. Campbell

Shaz motioned to Soroya, the mother, to sit on the other side of her daughter.

In a friendly, yet professional tone he said, "Hey, Georgiana, look at me."

She raised her head and looked at him through wet eyes.

"I know something's wrong, but I don't know exactly what. You gotta help me fix it, okay?"

Half a minute went by before she nodded and dried her eyes with a handful of tissue her mother pushed into her hand.

"Did Hussey try contacting you before you got here today?" he asked, referring to her former pimp.

She shook her head and bit her lip.

Shaz folded his hands. "Has he been in contact since I saw you last week?"

Georgiana nodded and started crying again. "H-he said he was coming to get me and that if I didn't come to him by this evening, I'd be sorry."

As she sobbed, he weighed what he should do. "Don't lie to me," he said, going back to what he thought was her current issue. "The man you passed coming in, d'you know him?"

Georgiana hiccupped as she dried her eyes, but her tears wouldn't stop coming.

Shaz raised his voice, but kept it well-modulated, to avoid startling Georgiana. "Elise."

When she appeared in the doorway, he said, "Water, please."

She spun away and came back to hand him a glass filled with cold water.

As the girl took a long sip, Shaz thought about how to pose his next question. He decided to forgo tactful and go for direct. The moment he eased the glass out of her hand and onto the table in front of them, he said, "That man, was he one of your clients?"

Avoiding his eyes, she nodded.

"Is there anything in particular you remember about him?"

Her tan complexion went ruddy and she winced. With her head turned away, she said, "He's very rough. He likes to bite."

As his stomach twisted, Shaz asked. "Did he recognize you?"

"I don't think so. He was on his phone."

No doubt updating his client with the news that Shaz wasn't about to roll over and make things easy on them.

"Can I ask you a couple more questions?'

When she whispered yes, he said, "What you did with him, did it take place in The Castle?"

Her reluctant nod made him sick to his stomach. Another thing he'd discovered about that place, which made him wonder if he'd be up to the task of unraveling all the crap that had gone on in Khalil's absence. All of this was a far cry from Khalil Germaine's original set up. Only God knew what other horrors the Kings would unearth if they kept digging.

"D'you know how many other girls were kept in that place and where they came from?"

Georgiana picked at her nail and mumbled. "From different places across the country and some from the Caribbean." She squinted as she concentrated. "Haiti, Jamaica, The Bahamas."

What Shaz needed to find out, he could ask Daron to investigate, so he patted Georgiana's hand. "Thanks. You've done good. And don't worry about Hussey. He won't be bothering you again."

"Are you sure?" she asked, in a wobbly voice. "He has people working for him."

"Trust me. I'll take care of it. Don't worry about him. I have better people working for me." He got to his feet. "Soraya, I think that's enough for today. Georgiana has been very helpful."

The girl's smile, as she rose, was all the encouragement he needed for his next move.

"Soraya, let's talk for a second." They walked to the far end of the room, close to the entrance. Looking her in the eyes, he said, "Does this guy, Hussey, know where you live?"

She shook her head. "I don't think so. Georgiana linked up with him when she was knocking heads with her friends from Chicago." She sighed and dragged both hands down her cheeks. "She's scared and ashamed because of how she used to act, but since she's been trapped in that place, she's changed." She glanced toward where Georgiana sat. "Please do all you can to keep her safe."

"You know I will." He faced the plate-glass door and lowered his voice as an idea took shape. "Do me a favor and wait here while I make a call. I'd prefer to know you're perfectly safe than to let you walk back into a bad situation."

Relief shone from Soraya's eyes, and she said, "Sure, I'll wait."

He strode back to his office and rang Dro's number. Shaz outlined the challenge and explained his concern, after which Dro promised to get back to him in a few minutes.

Shaz checked his email and was at the door when the phone rang. After a glance at the display, he smiled. "I may have to rename you Speedy Gonzales. That was lightning fast."

"This is what fixers do, come up with creative solutions. On the double."

Both men chuckled, then Dro said, "Have them wait there and I'll send someone. He'll transport them to their home to get whatever they need. We'll organize temporary housing until everything settles."

"Sounds good to me. They'll be waiting. Thanks."

When he gave Soraya the news, she nodded and let out a deep breath.

"Make yourself comfortable," he said. "Your escort will be here in a few minutes."

Her grateful smile pained his heart. He turned away and shoved both hands into his pockets. His fingers tangled in the chain and his hand fisted around the gold medallion of St. Joseph, patron saint of fathers and workers. Once again, he was reminded of the promises he made to himself at the start of his career and the sacrifices his family had made so he could help others.

"Shaz."

Elise's voice startled him, but he held his composure, turning to face her.

"I'm packing it in for the day." One of her perfectly arched brows chided him. "Don't stay here 'til midnight. Again."

"Look at you tryna tell me not to overwork myself. You must have gotten a life or something to be leaving this early." By his watch, it was five thirty. Half the time, he left Elise in office.

"Mind ya business," she said, going past him with her handbag.

He waved and chuckled. "Enjoy your evening."

"I definitely will," she said, pushing the glass door. She exchanged a few words with the security in the outer area before leaving the building.

Behind his desk, Shaz got Daron on the line.

"I'm beginning to think trouble is your middle name," Daron said by way of a greeting. "What's up?"

After a dry chuckle, Shaz revealed, "There's something I need you to arrange for me."

"I'm listening."

Shaz explained the situation with his young client. "From what I'm seeing, Bennett's lawyer is connected to that high-class outfit that caters to their customers' fantasies. Doesn't matter how far out their desires or needs are, The Elite Hub panders to them. Attorney-client privilege means I can't divulge what happened to my client or who she is, except to say she's underage. To cut to the chase, there's this guy, Hussey, that I need gone from her life, so she and her mother can return to their home."

"What are my limitations?"

"He's the scum of the earth, so frankly I don't even wanna know what you do with him. I just want him to leave this child alone."

"I'm on it," Daron said. "I'll have Luca pay him a visit."

Eyes on the painting on the wall across the room, Shaz asked, "Do I want to know who that is?"

"It's better that you don't."

As they chuckled, Shaz remembered his final request. "Those earrings that you developed for our womenfolk?"

"Yes?" Daron stayed silent until Shaz continued, "You don't give an inch, do you?"

"Generally? No. State your case or hold your peace."

"Those specialized earrings that you developed for us … I'm going to need two pairs."

"Not one?"

"Like I said, two. One is for a little girl. Coming off yesterday's incident, I'm taking no chances that anybody will try and grab this baby girl again."

After ending the call, Shaz pulled up the email Daron had sent via the secure network he'd created for the managing directors and Kings of The Castle. He scanned the reports on Bennett and Porter before suspicion took root in his mind. Something had been puzzling him about the man who followed him from the gym. Now that the alderman's business had come to him in the form of Milholland, Shaz knew exactly what had bothered him about the entire situation. Connections. Seen and unseen.

A grin crossed his face, as he thought about Daron. With the amount of information Shaz kept demanding, he'd start wondering about him. That's if he didn't already know or suspect that somehow, everything tied back to The Castle.

His phone rang, and his amusement faded.

The security he'd put on Camilla was calling.

CHAPTER 12

Shaz sat outside Miss Mabel's place, wondering if he'd made a mistake leaving his office. There was nothing unusual about Camilla coming to the restaurant, but Daniel had proven himself to be alert in the couple days since he'd been with Camilla, reporting in at least once every twenty-four hours. Along with another man, they cycled through twelve-hour shifts. Up to this moment, everything had been quiet.

Daniel stood in front of a plate glass window on the sidewalk, his attention focused inside the restaurant. Inconspicuous, except for his height, he stood a few inches taller than Shaz, who was 6'3. As Shaz approached, Daniel pulled the door open and entered the restaurant.

Shaz quickened his steps, hoping good sense would prevail long enough for him to prevent Camilla from doing anything impulsive. Daniel trailed her there after she blew out of the house. He was in two minds about to whether to follow her since she left the baby behind. The fact that another adult was in the house made the decision for Daniel.

A slew of purposeful steps took Shaz to the far end of the restaurant. Miss Mabel's Jamaican Joint hummed with Marley music and the wall behind the counter carried the colors of the Jamaican flag. The mahoe furniture, shaded lighting and muted chatter gave the place a warm atmosphere. After assessing the unfolding situation with Camilla, he backtracked to the counter. Miss Mabel opened the door from the kitchen and approached the cashier. The second she caught Shaz in her line of sight, she chuckled. "You come to pick up some dinner? We have Stewed Peas today, wit' pig's tail."

"Sounds good." He stepped in closer and spoke at a lower pitch. "D'you know Camilla is here?"

She frowned and scanned the restaurant's small eating area. "No, I talked to her about ten minutes ago. She's supposed to be at home."

"Well, she isn't." He leaned on the counter. "She's here."

Miss Mabel squawked, "What? Why?"

Shaz stepped to one side as a young woman in the cashier's line jostled him. "If you want to stop setting her off, please don't tell her stuff that will have her storming into your place of business."

Eyes round, Miss Mabel hauled her apron over her head and pulled off the hair net.

"Don't panic." Shaz stepped away from the counter. "Let me handle this."

Miss Mabel nodded, but shoved the items in her hand under the counter and approached the half door in the curved wooden surface.

Everything was normal where the customers were served, but in the secluded seating area to the left, the atmosphere was tense. The diners sitting to that side had stopped eating and were focused on the back of the alcove. Shaz couldn't see clearly around Daniel and the waiter who stood in his path. When Shaz touched Daniel's arm, he stepped out of the way.

Camilla stood with her back to them. Her voice was lowered and her arms folded, Camilla's rigid stance told Shaz she was intent on whatever she'd come to do.

Bennett sat facing Shaz and the features of the man Camilla was speaking with were hidden from him. He shifted sideways and his profile came into view. His skin was a deep mahogany and he wore a diamond stud. The bottom half of his face was covered by a beard. When he got to his feet, and Camilla took a step back, Shaz moved to stand behind her.

The realization hit Shaz then. The man she was arguing with was the father of her child. Ayanna was Camilla's child except for the almond-shaped eyes and wavy hair he now knew she inherited from her father.

"What you gonna do?" Camilla asked, as if she wasn't at least six inches shorter than the man she was challenging.

"Anything to get you out of my face and to stop embarrassing me," he snapped.

Camilla took a half step toward him. "You should have thought of that before—"

In a low, but commanding voice, Shaz said her name.

She barely glanced behind her before turning her attention back to Porter, who was dressed in a long-sleeve shirt and jeans. "Let me tell you something, you worthless pile of—"

"Camilla." Shaz put more volume into his voice.

This time, she turned. Only the slight widening of her eyes told Shaz he'd surprised her. "What are you doing here?"

"I'll give you one guess." His gaze swung between her and Porter.

Bennett walked around Camilla and stretched a hand toward Shaz.

He debated whether to shake the man's hand, but did what good manners dictated. "Alderman."

"It's always good to see you, Bostwick."

Raising one hand in a gesture that encompassed the room. Shaz said, "It's a surprise to see you here."

Bennett showed his teeth in a predatory grin. "I stay close to my constituents," he said, in a booming voice, as if making sure the entire restaurant heard each word, but his intended audience had gone back to eating their meals.

Shaz grunted and glanced at the table strewn with half empty glasses of beer and what he assumed was sour sop juice. "Seems an odd place to be canvassing for votes."

"Although I'm always on the job, there's life outside of my official capacity." Bennett's gaze swung between Shaz and Camilla. "So, what brings you here?"

"I'm a regular customer." He waited a beat before adding. "And since Miss Mabel told me my client was here, I took the opportunity to have a word with her."

With a pointed look, Camilla asked Shaz what he was doing.

He inclined his head toward her. "I need to talk with you. Now."

"I'm not finished here." She turned back toward Porter.

"Well, I'm done." He tried moving past her, but Camilla shifted toward him. He brushed by, bumping shoulders with her.

"Hey," Shaz planted himself in Porter's path. "That's not how you treat a lady."

"I'm trying to avoid a confrontation." He pointed at Bennett. "I came here to do business."

"Don't you dare refer to my daughter as any kind of business," Camilla hissed. "If you think I'm going to let you go through with this nonsense, you can guess again."

"You don't know what we were talking about." One side of the man's mouth curled in disgust "So, I'd suggest you mind *your* business."

"I'd say the lady has reason to be concerned."

Porter turned cool eyes on Shaz. "Who the hell are you anyway?"

Looking at Porter from head to heels, Shaz replied. "The man who's about to become your biggest nightmare."

Eyes on Camilla, Porter faked a smile. "Who is this gentrified clown?"

Shaz stood straight, shoving both hands into the pockets of his tailored pants. "You won't be so full of crap when we get done with you. Remember that."

He stepped out of Bennett's way. "If I were you, I'd be on my way, too."

The Alderman shifted and looked around them as if suddenly aware they were again the central focus in the room. "Derrick, we were almost finished so—"

Porter held his ground, his face twisted in a frown. His mouth opened as if he was about to say something else, but Daniel edged in front of Shaz, who'd forgotten he was there.

"Oh, so it's like that, huh?" Porter eased past Daniel, while throwing a glare at Shaz. "Last I heard, this place was public and meant for *all* customers."

He stepped past Shaz and almost ran into Miss Mabel. "Nice to see you, Miss Mabel."

"Dat's more dan I can say about you." She rested both hands on her wide hips. "And dis place, as you called it, is not meant for *all* and sundry. I have standards. And by di way young man, when you start actin' like my niece's enemy, dat makes you *my* enemy."

She turned her eyes on Bennett, who was trying to get past the group. "If I were you, I'd be careful of the company you keep."

Neither man dared ask which of them she meant. As they rushed through the door, she muttered. "Should kick the two of you out on your …"

A wave of chuckles rose from those seated close to the plate glass windows and drowned her words.

Shaz hid a grin and dismissed Daniel with a tilt of the head. When his attention went to Camilla, Shaz assumed a serious expression. "Have you had dinner?"

"Huh?"

Her response told him that was the last thing she expected him to say. "I asked if you ate."

She shook her head. "We have food at home, so don't worry about me."

"Wait for me," he said, cupping her elbow. After paying for his food, thanking Miss Mabel, and reassuring her he'd take Camilla home, they left the restaurant.

At the sidewalk, Shaz opened the SUV for Camilla to get in. While they locked the seatbelts, he thought about what to say to Camilla. He decided on a direct approach. "Did you think about what you were doing when you ran out of the house?"

She stared through the windshield but said nothing.

"I don't get why you always choose to run headlong into danger." He stared at her, but she still refused to look at him. "It's like you have no sense of self preservation."

After she released a sigh, she said, "When it concerns Ayanna, I do whatever it takes to protect her."

"Tearing over here to confront these men isn't necessary." He sat sideways in the seat. "If you'd just let me do my job, things would go a lot smoother."

"Sometimes, nothing speaks louder than direct action," she shot back.

"And *sometimes,* I think reasoning with you is a waste of breath."

Camilla cut him with a bad look. "Are you saying I'm irrational?"

Rubbing his forehead, Shaz chose his words with care. "No, what I'm saying is—"

Her phone interrupted his answer. She pulled it out of the small bag she carried across her body and put it to her ear. "Yeah, Stacey."

As she listened, her eyes widened. "Is it anybody we know?"

She grabbed Shaz's arm. "Drive."

"What happened?" He put the SUV in gear and stepped on the gas.

Camilla didn't answer immediately, then she said to the caller, "Whatever you do, please don't let Ayanna out of your sight."

As he engaged the SUV's audio system, Shaz cast a glance at Camilla. She was still on the phone and sat forward as if that would make the Alfa Romeo go faster.

Daniel answered his phone, and Shaz said, "Trouble at base. Hurry back."

"I'll be there in a couple of minutes."

Glancing sideways, Shaz asked, "So, are you going to tell me what's happening at the house?"

Camilla raked her teeth over her lips a couple of times as her eyes filled. Blinking hard, she said, "Stacey said there's a couple of guys across the street. They came when I left and she thinks they're watching the house."

CHAPTER 13

Stacey's wide eyes cased him from his locs to the Italian leather shoes covering his feet. Then her gaze shifted to Camilla, who rushed forward to take Ayanna from her arms. Other than the family resemblance around the eyes and mouth, they were different women. Stacey was short and plump like Miss Mabel, with cocoa skin and a headful of braids.

The thick Latino muscleman from next door, who escorted her across the walkway that separated the houses, left a moment ago.

After kissing Ayanna and hugging her close, Camilla introduced them.

Ignoring the speculation in Stacey's gaze, Shaz asked, "Did you get a good look at any of the men?"

"I did better than that." Smiling, Stacey whipped a phone out of the back pocket of her jeans. "I got pictures."

With his brows raised, Shaz moved to the doorway and took the phone. "You had time to take photos?"

"Don't worry," she said, "I just wanted them to know who they were messing with."

He could have said safety and the baby's well-being should have been her first consideration, but didn't.

Stacey pointed toward the next property and grinned. "When Miguel came outside with that gun, they peeled off like the hounds of hell were on their tails."

When neither Shaz or Camilla laughed, her merriment died.

Shaz reeled off his telephone number and asked her to send him the pictures. He'd shoot them at Daron and ask him to get some background on the men.

When they sat in the living room, Stacey's gaze homed in on him. "So, who are you to Cam?"

"Her friend."

"My lawyer."

His eyes met Camilla's over Ayanna's head. Evidently, her privacy was mega-important. He'd go along with her wishes, but they needed to have a conversation. Their relationship had changed, but he didn't want to enter a situation where they were both headed in different directions.

"D'you know how long those guys were outside?" he asked.

"They sat there for twenty minutes and they were looking directly at Momma's house." A sheepish expression took over her face. "When they pulled up, someone also passed by on a motorbike. I checked the time. That's how I know."

"You're more observant than most people." He nodded, encouraging her to continue.

"They wouldn't take their eyes off the house, so I opened the front door." She squinted in concentration. "When the driver stepped out of the car, I knew it was time to move."

Frowning, she asked Camilla. "I know Momma ain't involved in nothin', so I wanna know why they came to watch her house."

"You know I'm as straight as an arrow." Shrugging, Camilla added, "Maybe it has something to do with Derrick."

Shaz had to give her props for her acting skills. The anxiety he'd felt coming off her the first time they met now shrouded Camilla. Looking at her, though, he couldn't tell she was worried. He opened his mouth, but Stacey was speaking again.

"I don't know what you saw in that good-for-nothing loser. But if he had anything to do with this, Momma will sort him out. You know how she feels about him."

What they faced was no laughing matter, but Stacey's speech was reminiscent of her mother and made Shaz smile. As Stacey got to her feet, she said, "Anyway, I gotta go. Talk to you later, Cam. If you need me, you know the number."

"Thanks, cuz."

The two women hugged, then Camilla followed Stacey to the door. When it closed behind her, Camilla leaned on the wood looking at him while Ayanna babbled in her arms.

"I try to keep a low profile," Camilla said.

Wearing a wry smile, Shaz rubbed his beard. "You don't say."

He wasn't into the social scene in Jamaica, nor did he follow world travel, but now and then, he checked out her blog, which had made her something of a minor celebrity with Caribbean people. As far as he knew, Camilla had visited as many places as she could where she didn't need a visa. She kept her readers entertained with little-known information about the places her adventures took her. Of course, he also noticed the logos of prominent companies he assumed sponsored her blog.

Laughing, Camilla set Ayanna on her feet. "I know what you're thinking."

He shared her humor with an answering grin. "You're a mind reader now, Cam?"

Her laughter faded as she moved toward him, shaking her head a little. "Nope, but I can see the wheels turning in your brain. You're thinking, how can she say that when she's been modeling and has that blog."

"That's right. I see that even with family, you're tight as a clam."

She grabbed for Ayanna, who staggered toward Shaz with her arms held out. The little girl giggled and ran to Shaz, who encouraged her with a beckoning motion.

Ayanna beamed up at him and squealed when he lifted her onto his leg.

"I gotta admit," Camilla said, as she sat next to him, "I've spent a lot of time inside my head since things started going wrong with Derrick."

"How long have you guys not been an item?" he asked. "It's weird that I haven't asked before now and I question everything. Too much going on, I guess."

"We broke up just before I discovered I was pregnant. The only reason we're in contact now is because I have to be here for Ayanna's treatment."

"Hmmm." Shaz had been dissecting the situation and sifting through what seemed to be an escalating problem. From what he saw, Derrick was trying to rid himself of responsibility, including any child support claims.

Shaz had arrived at a solution, which he had to sell to Camilla.

Ayanna tugged a handful of his locs and he gently tapped her under the chin. He raised his head and caught Camilla eyeing him with an analytical expression. Their eyes met and her gaze softened.

"I have an idea," he said.

Threading one hand through her hair, she sat facing him. "Why do I think I'm not going to like whatever comes next."

Ayanna grabbed the end of his tie and loosened it further. When his attention went back to Camilla, he said, "I think you should move to my place in The Castle."

Wrinkling her face, Camilla pulled back her head. "That place looks like an ivory tower."

"Where you won't have to worry about Ayanna's safety."

Dragging a hand through her hair again, she asked, "What am I gonna do there all day?"

His tone was gentle but insistent. "The same thing you do here."

She moved her head side to side. "How am I going to get around to do my business when I'm stuck all the way over there?"

"That, you don't have to worry about, I can arrange—"

A stubborn mask descended over her features. "I don't like that *I can arrange* part."

When he attempted to speak, Camilla held up one hand. "D'you realize just how much stuff you've been taking care of for me? When you're used to doing for yourself, it makes you feel powerless when someone else is trying to do everything for you."

He hid his frustration behind his calm words. "All I'm trying to do is keep you safe."

She squeezed his arm. "Thank you, but this is my problem and I need to work it out my way."

"I get that, but I'm not leaving you out on a limb to deal with Bennett by yourself."

The baby tugged at his locs again and pulled one of them toward her mouth.

"No, Ayanna." Camilla scooted closer and lifted the toddler onto her lap.

The baby made protesting sounds and grabbed another handful of his hair, examining it and chattering to herself.

"Trust me, I'm grateful for that," Camilla said, resting her head on his shoulder. "But I can't allow you to move me into your place like I'm some kind of concubine. What will Auntie think?"

"Your aunt has never struck me as narrow minded." His arm slipped around her waist. "She'll think I'm doing exactly what I'm doing, which is protecting you."

With her arm wrapped around his, Camilla kissed his jaw. "I love you for that, but the answer is still no."

He looked down at her as all traces of indecision drained from him. "You win, Camilla. For now. But, believe me when I say, if anything else jumps off, I don't care how small it is, I'm moving you into the Castle."

"I—"

"My mind is made up. Better to be safe than picking up the pieces. As my granny used to say, prevention is better than a cure." He tipped her chin toward him. "Are we clear?"

She looked away from him, then sighed. "I suppose so. I know you're trying to help."

"Arrgggh."

Ayanna's outburst made both of them laugh, and Camilla let her down on the floor.

"See," Shaz chuckled. "Ayanna understands what time of day it is."

He got to his feet. "Daniel's outside, so you'll be fine. If you have a problem, no matter how small, call me."

At the door, she turned her face up to his. "Of course. We'll be all right, though."

The worry in her dark-brown eyes negated her words and silently, Shaz cursed her pride and stubborn streak. Since Camilla wouldn't listen to him, he'd do what was necessary to keep her safe.

Cupping her cheek, he brought his lips down to hers. Before he could deepen their kiss, a pair of tiny hands grabbed him by the pants. Ayanna waved at him to pick her up.

As he swung her into the air, she showed her tiny, pearly-white teeth in delighted laughter.

"I hear you, little one."

She patted his cheeks and yammered while he handed her to Camilla.

"I guess that takes care of that," he said, and kissed Camilla's forehead. "I'll touch base with you later."

He walked through the door and was about to close it behind him when Camilla's voice stopped him.

"Shaz."

His mouth tipped up in answer to her smile. "Yeah?"

She stepped onto the verandah's wooden surface and crooked a finger at him, a mischievous quality to her smile. When he was close enough, she held the back of his head with her free arm and pulled him in for a kiss.

Camilla wasn't playing. She dominated the kiss, going deep and keeping him connected to her with a firm grip. Then her touch was soft and delicate, making him yearn to make love to her. But that would have to wait. For now, he'd make do with what she was offering.

Her smile was sweet when they separated. Before she turned away, she placed one last kiss on his chin. "Bye, love."

Moving slow and easy, Camilla went back inside the house with the baby waving at him from her hip.

A satisfied smile pulled at his lips. Their coming together was going to be like fireworks.

He pulled in a deep breath and faced the road. The sight of the Jetta across the street was reassuring, but the weight in his gut warned him that they hadn't seen the last of whoever was stalking Camilla and her family.

CHAPTER 14

This is downright weird.

What was the likelihood that two days after seeing one sex trafficking victim, another one should pop up on his radar tied to the same entity? If he didn't understand what was going on within The Castle's walls, he'd think it was a mere coincidence.

Soraya told the woman across the desk about him. From Marva's accent, Shaz knew she was also Jamaican. She'd been living and working in the States for some time. From Georgiana, she got a message that her daughter, who resided in Jamaica, was inside The Castle and needed help.

Looking up from his notes, Shaz asked, "How is it possible for her to be here when you left her in Jamaica?"

Marva shrugged, bit her ragged nails, then scratched her scalp. "I don' know. I left her with my sister, but she said Nicole bruk out." She winced and continued, "Sorry, I mean she started acting like she's a woman and she told my sister she joined some kind of dancing club with girls her age and younger. She heard the better dancers would get picked to go on tour abroad. My sister didn't believe her."

Pen poised, Shaz looked at the lined paper. "You said she was fourteen?"

"Yes, last month."

As her tears came, Shaz's stomach lurched. Fourteen. He didn't want to think about what that meant. Some perverts thought the younger the girl, the better. Milholland came to mind, and Shaz barely stopped himself from swearing. These men thought their money made them invincible, that they could buy anything. Including human flesh.

A snippet of his conversation with Soraya came to mind. Coincidences were few in his world, so Shaz leaned forward, laser focused on the woman across the desk. "Which community did your daughter live in?"

"Waterford."

The same place Soraya had mentioned they were from originally. There had to be a connection and if there was one, he'd find it.

"Did she mention any names to your sister? Persons who were involved in the dancing club? Anyone who befriended her before she disappeared?"

She thought for a moment, asked him for the password for his Wi-Fi and shot off a message. In two minutes, she provided him with three names received from her sister. She also sent him pictures of her daughter, which he immediately downloaded and sent to his email to distribute to the Kings, who were helping him.

With a hand pressed to her lips, Marva closed her eyes and sniffed. "Nicole is not a bad girl. She just followed bad company and got caught up in something that … oh, God."

Shaz allowed her to weep, but went to the credenza and brought the box of tissue to her.

With a trembling hand, she removed a few. When she wiped her eyes and blew her nose, she stuffed the crumpled paper in her handbag. "Thanks for taking my case. Soraya said you're the best. Please get my daughter out of that place, Mr. Bostwick."

"I'll do my best," he said, as he guided her to the door. "As soon as I have an update, I'll be in touch with you."

When he slid back into his seat, Shaz pulled his laptop forward and wrote an email to Phillip Denham, a cousin on his mother's side who lived in Jamaica. Phillip had moved up in the police force and would be able to get him the information he needed quickly.

Shaz also attached the photos of the girl. The minute he hit send, his phone rang. Grinning, he put the cellular to his ear. "Mom, what's popping?"

"Boy, in case you forgot, yo mama ain't your friend. You young'uns don't have no respect."

Her use of double negatives still tickled him and he chuckled. "You love me anyway. So, what d'you need?"

"I'm having a picnic on Saturday."

"Where?" he asked, as if he didn't know.

"In the backyard, of course." Her tone lightened. "You know I'm not going anywhere where we might run the risk of being arrested for having a picnic while Black."

"You watch too much television," he said, crossing his feet on the edge of the desk.

"And you obviously spend so much time in that office, you don't realize what's happening out here in these streets." She laughed at her use of slang. "Anyway, you romp too much. In your line of work, you can't not know what's going on in our world."

She muffled the phone, said a few words, then came back to Shaz. "So, am I seeing you?"

They both knew there was one answer to that, but he teased her. "I'll see if I can work it into my schedule."

"If you don't want me to disown you, you better bring your narrow tail here by eleven o' clock. And by the way, I'm running low on that Sangster's Coconut Rum Cream."

After a belly laugh, Shaz responded in a British accent, "Your wish is my command, Queen Paula."

"And don't you forget it."

They laughed again and she said, "Do me a favor and bring Mabel's niece with you. I've seen her at church, but didn't get a chance to say more than two dozen words to her. I hear the two of you are doing more than business."

"You old women do like to 'labrish' and get all up in people's business. I'll see if I can persuade her."

In a sweet voice, Paula chided him. "If we don't gossip, or labrish as you call it, how can we keep up with all the stuff you're doing since you never visit or tell me anything."

He sputtered in protest. "Mom, I-I was over there—"

"Weeks ago."

"What about you and Dad's plan to sail into the sunset?"

"That's part of why I want you over here, so stop questioning me. See you on Saturday."

With that, she was gone. Despite her jokes, ensuring that he came to the family home for a reason only she knew, was the entire point of his mother's call. Shaz had learned that studying Paula Bostwick would take more time than he'd ever have to spare. Teddy Bostwick had been married to her for forty-two years and still couldn't grasp all her idiosyncrasies.

Shaz swung his legs off the desk and walked to the wall where his certificates were displayed. He was uneasy. Almost as if he was going to receive news he wouldn't welcome. Although he was settling into his role as a managing director at The Castle, he was disgusted by the dark underbelly of the expansive property. With so many deprived and hurting people in the world, it was hard to understand how those with the ability to help, used their resources to inflict more pain on the unfortunate. Soraya and Marva were struggling mothers who were trying to better their families, but that left their daughters vulnerable.

He moved to the desk and pulled the laptop closer. Philip had already responded with a return email and a file attached. The document was a police report on a raid conducted in the Waterford community. He included a dossier that carried names and corresponding photos of suspects tied to a human trafficking ring. As he scanned the list of names, he came across two that didn't have pictures, but it didn't matter. He knew the identity of one of the missing suspects.

He eased back in his seat, rubbing his chin and neck in turn. When his thoughts wouldn't settle, he walked around the office threading his fingers through the chain in his pocket. He sat again and after studying the document a second time, closed the laptop and decided to go home.

His recent move to his own suite at The Castle put him farther away from Camilla, whose presence would have been welcome, but she'd vetoed that.

Tonight, he'd comb through the adoption agency's records and also pull information on The Elite Hub. That was one of *the* most exclusive gentlemen's clubs within The Castle, and a place to start turning over stones. He'd share what he found out with Mariano "Reno" DeLuca.

Reno was the board member with responsibility for matters to do with suspected trafficking of girls and women through the Castle. He worked hand in hand with Daron.

Where Daron provided mad skill with the intelligence and technical side of things, Reno was passionate about protecting victims. He was methodical and his safe house had an exemplary reputation. Shaz had no doubt that if he found anything underhanded, Reno would do the necessaries to get the missing girl out of that exclusive club.

While Shaz was in the middle of shrugging into his jacket, the door opened wider.

The man standing on the other side bared his teeth in a sharkish grin. "Seems like I came at a bad time."

CHAPTER 15

Bennett stepped inside the office, still wearing that deceptive smile.

"Your timing isn't the best." Shaz picked up the laptop and slid it into the protective sleeve.

"This won't take long," Bennett said, advancing into the office.

Shaz didn't sit, nor did he invite the Alderman to take a seat.

The lack of a welcome didn't faze the politician. He slid both hands into his pockets and cleared his throat. "I want to make you an offer."

"Let's hear it," Shaz said, mirroring the older man's pose.

"As I explained, my wife has become attached to Ayanna—"

"I hate to be rude, but I distinctly remember telling you that baby was not up for adoption, much less discussion."

Bennett raised one hand. "Hear me out. Please."

"I'm listening," Shaz said in a less than inviting tone.

"Like I said, Lori-Anne loves that little girl. Finding out she won't be getting Ayanna is going to break her heart. We can afford to give her the treatment and care she needs for her heart condition." He paused and studied Shaz as if gauging his every reaction. "With the expense of treating her, plus the tragedy that might occur if she doesn't receive proper care, I'm suggesting that you look the other way where this adoption is concerned."

Bennett stepped in closer, lowering his voice and speaking in a wheedling tone. "Let us adopt the baby. Give her the life she deserves. If you let this happen, I promise there will be a huge reward in it for you."

"Let me understand this." Shaz lifted his locs over the collar of his jacket and folded both arms. "You're saying this baby means so much to your wife, you're willing to *buy* her out from under her mother's nose?"

Bennett winced, but recovered quickly. "Our action will benefit the little girl."

"No." Shaz stabbed the air with a finger. "This thing you're trying to arrange will benefit *you* and *your* wife."

The Alderman shrugged. "A man will do anything to keep his woman happy."

Shaz nodded his agreement. "That, I understand, but within the limits of decency."

"No matter what price he has to pay," Bennett added in a more strident tone.

Shaz made a mental note to talk to the security about letting persons into the office, in Elise's absence, without advance warning. "Here's what I don't understand. First you cajole, then you threaten, and now you want to buy my integrity?"

"It's not that serious." Bennett waved his hand in a dismissive way. "That young woman can have another baby. My wife is infertile. We'd be willing to give Ms. Gibson a generous compensation package, *if* she agrees to give up Ayanna."

The man's cool tone—as if he were talking about buying produce from a supermarket, or food from a restaurant—made Shaz's blood boil. Heat crawled from his neck into his face. He was certain his skin was turning a mottled red-brown shade. Still, he held his silence.

"She'd be better off letting us raise Ayanna as our own." With a self-satisfied smirk, Bennett concluded, "Matter of fact, it would benefit *all of us* if Ms. Gibson signs on the dotted line."

Shaz itched to say something so vile the Alderman's ears would burn, but he remembered something Khalil had taught him years ago. *Never descend to the level of desperate people. Taking the high road never hurt anyone. It builds character, especially under difficult circumstances.*

"You have everything worked out to the letter, it seems." Shaz picked up the laptop, then met Bennett's gaze. "Hear me and hear me well. There will *not* be an adoption where this child is concerned."

Bennett drew a sharp breath, as if Shaz's response was unexpected. He regrouped quickly. "Are you aware Ayanna was born in the United States?"

Shaz stood to his full height. "I'm perfectly aware of that. Your point?"

"That gives her a legal right to be here." An evil light gleamed in his eyes. "The mother, not so much."

Tucking the laptop under one arm, Shaz stepped away from the desk. "Are you trying to tell me something?"

Bennett rocked back and forth on his heels. "With her visa issues, it won't be too long before she's wedged between a rock and a very hard place."

After pushing the executive chair into position behind his desk, Shaz unleashed what was in his mind. "Only a vulture preys on the misfortune of others."

Bennett's face blanched, then he scowled. "How dare you?"

"No. How dare *you* come to my office making veiled threats against my client. You think your money and power make you invincible?"

Slowly, Bennett shook his head "Not at all, but having cash to care for this little girl makes a big difference between who wins and who loses."

As he walked toward the door, he said, "We can do this the easy way, or we can fight tooth and nail to the … deportation. Whichever you prefer is fine with me."

"And I'll tell you the same thing I told you last time." Shaz stopped in the middle of the room. "There won't be an adoption. Find. Another. Baby."

Bennett filled the doorway, pointing at Shaz. "One thing I've learned in life is that nothing is impossible once you have the money to buy it. Nothing."

"We'll see about that, Mr. Bennett."

Over his shoulder, Bennett shot back. "We should be working on the same side since we're both directors at The Castle."

"I'd think so, too," Shaz drawled, "except you seem to be on the opposite side of the fence. And get it right, I'm a managing member with voting shares, who outranks you."

Bennett faced Shaz once more, piercing him with a sharp gaze. "It still benefits you to do the wise thing."

"My client's interest is my priority, not what you or your wife want. Let's get that clear."

A nasty smile curved the Alderman's mouth. "From what I hear, Ms. Gibson seems to be more than your client."

His words stopped Shaz cold. He didn't scare easy, but he also didn't want people keeping tabs on his personal business. Make it worse, he didn't yet know who had eyes on Camilla and Ayanna.

"What I do on my own time is none of your business."

"Oh, but it is," Bennett taunted. "There's got to be something wrong with a lawyer fraternising with his client."

In the Alderman's eyes, Shaz saw determination and awareness of his power. Bennett had another guess coming if he thought Shaz cared about threats, overt or otherwise. "Our business is finished, Mr. Bennett."

"Not until I get what I want."

Crossing the tiles to stand in front of Bennett, Shaz squared his shoulders. "Read my lips. I do not bow to pressure. Ever."

"We'll see about that." Bennett scoffed and marched into the reception area.

"Be careful how you come into my space and threaten me," Shaz drawled, "because you might not be able to handle the repercussions."

Bennett spun and pointed at Shaz, his finger shaking in his fury. "You'll learn that I'm not a man to be trifled with. I get whatever I want. Always."

With a smile in place and an even tone, Shaz replied, "Always is a strong word from a weak adversary. Remember that."

CHAPTER 16

Reno sat back and patted his stomach. "We should have done this the other way around."

"What do you mean?" Daron asked, easing away from the dinner table.

"I know exactly what he's talking about." Dro's dimples appeared as he added, "All of this rib-sticking food is going to put us to sleep and we won't finish what we came to do."

"Just wake me when you're ready to hit the road," Grant said, laughing.

Dro nudged him playfully in the side. "No sleep for me, means no sleep for you, my brother."

They'd made short work of the spread of Curried Goat, Oxtails and Beans, Fried Chicken, and Ackee & Saltfish with rice and peas, fried plantains, and lightly-fried roasted breadfruit since they sat at Shaz's dining table. Miss Mabel had topped off the entrées with June plum juice and lemonade. The delivery man also dropped off individually packaged servings of sweet potato pudding and carrot cake. Then, he whisked away the two women Miss Mabel sent to plate their meals, as though she thought Shaz wouldn't do it properly.

She was right. All of this mouth-watering deliciousness meant decorum went straight out of the window. Without help, they would have fallen on the food like starving savages.

After the discoveries he made about Bennett's business and Porter's history between Wednesday and Thursday, Shaz invited Daron, Dro, Reno, and Grant to have dinner at his suite on Friday. They all came straight from work and had shrugged off their jackets and sat with their sleeves rolled back and assorted devices at their elbows.

"So, what's this about The Elite Hub?" Grant asked.

"Their name came up because of two of my clients." Shaz eased away his empty plate. "One of them escaped while being transported from wherever the girls are kept, to the clubhouse—"

"Hold up." Reno raised both hands, his green eyes intense. "What girls? Are you saying what I think you're saying?"

Giving a sharp nod, Shaz inhaled deeply. "Somewhere within this *labyrinth* of interconnected clubs and businesses—and in doing my investigations of the systems within The Castle, that's the best word to describe what I've found—there are girls who have been trafficked."

Reno turned a laser-sharp gaze on Shaz. "I'd say you're kidding me, but since you're as serious as a judge about to hand down a lifetime sentence, I know you're not joking."

Shaz scanned the face of each man at the dinner table. "All of this relates to one specific case I'm handing. The reason I brought you here this evening was to ask for your help and give you a heads-up before Monday's meeting. I don't want to take up the entire agenda with this. By then, I know you all will have done your own research on top of the information I've shared with you from Daron and Grant."

Here Shaz chuckled. "Any day now, Daron will stop answering my calls, but he's been giving me access to information on certain members, plus data I won't ask how he acquired."

Daron pulled an imaginary zipper across his lips.

The men laughed, then went silent when Shaz continued speaking. "Grant has been good enough to bring me up to date on who holds what shares and the ownership structure of The Hub and New Visions."

"So, what do you need from us before Monday's pow wow?" Dro asked, crossing one slack-covered leg over the other.

"Linkages." Shaz said, eyeing each of them in turn. "Mainly

between the adoption agency and The Hub. Seems to me that one name keeps popping up, which makes me wonder if Khalil's attempt to turn the whole shebang right side up, might not be enough cause for this individual to have been part of the assassination attempt. Trust me when I say he's involved with some seedy characters."

A tropical instrumental flooded the dining room. The men shot questioning gazes at Shaz, who got to his feet. "Relax. It's the doorbell."

They erupted in laughter.

"I don't know what we're gonna do with you," Dro quipped, shaking his head.

"There's nothing like having an island vibe flowing through my crib. Sets the mood, you know?" Shaz threw the words over his shoulder as he went to the get the door.

He welcomed back the two women he'd requested from The Castle's stable of housekeeping staff to clean up after them. When they filed into the kitchen ahead of him, Shaz hung back in the doorway. "Guys, let's move the discussion to the living room.

After the men went past him, Shaz closed the door between the dining and sitting areas. The walls of his suite were soundproof, plus equipped with Daron's anti-spyware devices so there was no danger of their business being spread through gossip. Thanks to Dro and their technical guru, each of them had their suites retrofitted with high-tech equipment that wasn't immediately obvious to the naked eye.

His brothers took seats around the low table decorated with patterned translucent glass that matched the blue accent wall at the far end of the living room. The sectional chairs came in a rich navy, with plump blue and white cushions. Shaz claimed his favorite seat, a curved half-sofa made to fit one person comfortably or two in intimate contact.

"Anything to drink?" he asked, tipping his head sideways. "The bar's over there."

"Are you for real?" Dro asked. "You stuff us to the gills, then want to ply us with drinks, too? No thanks, bro."

"And so say all of us," Grant added, but eyed the bar as if he'd change his mind later. "Anyway, tell us what exactly you need from us."

"My concern is that New Visions may be handling underhanded adoptions." He quickly updated them on Camilla's case, adding, "Where there's one, there are bound to be more. Since you're responsible for illegal deals and such on the property, you'll be able to tell us if their transactions stand up to scrutiny."

Hands clasped around his phone, Reno sat forward. "I'm assuming that you need me, in tandem with Daron, to turn over every stone inside The Castle to find these girls you mentioned."

"You got it." Shaz nodded, then turned his attention to Dro. "I have a feeling there's more than meets the eye with those two entities I mentioned. Over the years, I've learned to trust my instincts. Where there are embers, there's always fire."

"That's it then?" Reno asked. "If ya'll don't mind. I have to be somewhere else later this evening."

Shaz was certain 'somewhere else' had Zuri Okusanya's name all over it.

"That's it for me, too," Shaz said. "I know you all have places to be and people to see, so I won't keep you."

"Sounds good." Daron also got to his feet and picked up his tablet.

Grant and Reno followed suit. "We'll get back with you tomorrow."

"Appreciate it," Shaz said as they exchanged handshakes and man hugs.

Daron was the last to retrieve his jacket from the closet near the entrance to the suite. From an inner pocket, he pulled out a flat, gold gift box and handed it to Shaz.

"What are you two up to?" Grant asked, eyeing them with the same suspicion in his voice.

"Whatever you're thinking, you're wrong for that." Daron gave Grant and Reno a cool look. "Mind your business."

"And scrub your brain with carbolic soap and steel wool, too," Shaz added, with a cheeky grin.

Before walking over the threshold, Daron said, "I've included instructions on how to activate the devices inside."

"I'm grateful." Shaz dipped his head and put a hand over his heart, acknowledging the gift and how quickly Daron had moved to honor a request that could mean the difference between Camilla and Ayanna's harm and safety.

A half smile accompanied Daron's words. "You're welcome, but this is part of my role in protecting the brotherhood."

Shaz had to admit it was reassuring to have a network of professional brothers who could access some of the items he couldn't, even with his connections. That fact made him rest a bit easier whenever his mind strayed to Camilla and his other clients. Whoever had them on their radar would be no match for the group of men working in his corner.

Hands in his pockets, Shaz turned back toward the living room. As he did, the women emerged from the kitchen.

"We've taken care of everything Mr. Boswick," the older one advised.

Their pale blue and white garb reminded him of maids' uniforms he'd seen on television programs when he was growing up. He didn't know who ran the housekeeping business at The Castle but they needed to be brought into the present.

He gave both of them a generous tip and wished them a good night after acknowledging their thanks.

On the way to his bedroom, Shaz pulled his shirt from his pants and slid his phone off the center table. The hour was still early, so he rang Miss Mabel's cell.

She carried it in her apron pocket when she wasn't at the stove, because she didn't want to miss calls from customers or family.

"Good night, Shaz," she said at the top of her voice. "Everyt'ing was to ya liking?"

"Everything was delicious. You outdid yourself."

"Boy, ya certainly have a sweet mouth. But thank ya for saying so." She cackled. "I need to make sure Camilla knows all of your specialties."

He chuckled, but didn't comment because if he did, Miss Mabel and his mother would take it as license to orchestrate some moves on his behalf that he was capable of making on his own.

"I see ya keeping ya love life a secret, but dat's all right." She laughed at her own joke, then asked, "Ya needed anything in particular?"

"Just wanted to thank you," he said, sitting on the side of the bed.

"Miss Paula raised you right, young boy." She waited a few seconds as if giving him room to speak. In the next breath, she added, "I'll see you on Monday."

"Yes, save me some roast beef," he said, "and by the way, I needed to ask you a question."

"Go on. I knew there was something." Her laughter was hearty and came at full blast through the speaker. "Aunt Mabel wasn't born big."

Shaz grunted in acknowledgement of the old saying that meant she was much smarter than she appeared, while frowning at the royal blue accent wall. "This is about Camilla. I've talked to her, but haven't seen her since Wednesday."

He left space for Miss Mabel to fill in what he sensed while talking to Camilla on the phone today. Something wasn't right. She wouldn't admit anything was wrong, but his instincts hadn't failed him yet. She'd been withdrawn, then sharp, when he tried pulling her out of her mood.

"Camilla is my sister's own self. Secretive and mad as hell sometimes. Love to have her own way as old people would say. Ya right doh." She breathed hard into the phone. "She's been planning … for what I don't know. Glad you sniffed that out. Always knew ya was smart. Dat's why I asked ya to take her case. Dat and something else."

He didn't ask what that thing was because he suspected he already knew. Miss Mabel had been trying to hook him up for months, saying he needed a woman to cook for him and fatten him up. Not once did it occur to her that he trained and conditioned his body so he could eat whatever he wanted and not gain weight.

Shaz rose from the mattress and paced the area around the king-size bed. "Has she said anything to give you any idea of what she's up to?"

"No, but Camilla's been acting like Secret Squirrel these past couple of days, so I know she's up to something. I swear she has the blood of them runaway Maroons in her veins." She sighed at the reference to the runaway African slaves who battled and won two major wars against British soldiers in the 1700s. "Ya have a plan, young boy?"

"Maybe, but don't let me down, Miss Mabel. You can't say a word."

"I can be as secretive as the next woman." She gave a low cackle. "So secretive, I didn't tell you or Camilla that I figured ya have dat boy watching my house like we're in a James Bond movie."

A chuckle escaped from Shaz and he stopped, focused on an abstract painting in varying shades of blue—which reminded him of the Jamaican Blue Mountains. "I apologize, but it was necessary for a number of reasons."

Miss Mabel commiserated with him. "It's all right. I know ya only did it to protect her."

He stopped in front of the huge bay window, staring into the dark.

"That boy, Ayanna's father, needs a doctor to examine his head. Anyway, do what ya have to do to keep Camilla and my grandniece from that good-for-nothing devil's spawn. Only God can tell why she even looked in his direction."

When Shaz thought she wouldn't stop grousing, Miss Mabel, threw in a farewell. "Anyhow, I can't stand here chatting with ya all night. The customers can't serve themselves."

As he unlaced his shoes and went to the closet, he said, "Take care of yourself, Miss Mabel."

"Do the same for my niece," she shot back. "Sometimes I think that girl needs saving from herself."

Her words sent a shiver down his spine, but he swept it aside. He pulled his hair up in a heavy man bun, stripped off his clothes, and stepped into the warm spray of the shower. The stress of the week knotted his muscles and he'd missed his workout on Wednesday. He wound his head in a slow circle, reassuring himself he didn't need to worry. Daniel was in place and if Camilla didn't elude him and put herself at risk, Shaz could rest easy. The thought would have been reassuring, if he'd been dealing with any woman except Camilla.

CHAPTER 17

Shaz was beyond ready for Bostwick Construction business to be finalized. Roman had spoken with him earlier in the day and still refused to accept Shaz's decision. Helping people nagivate the pitfalls of moving to this country was his speciality and that's where he intended to focus his efforts in the foreseeable future.

His gaze shifted to Camilla. If she hadn't already wowed him, Shaz would have been worried his marital status was in danger. They arrived at his parents' house just over an hour ago, and Paula Bostwick had cornered Camilla the way she would a long-lost friend. Paula apologized for not seeking her out after Sunday service and hugged Camilla. The older woman also embraced Ayanna, who chattered as if she'd also found a new buddy. Ayanna hadn't let up since then. She tottered among the adults, cute as a doll in a yellow dress and matching sandals. Paula picked her up at every opportunity, as if Roman hadn't already made her a grandmother twice.

Paula had ensured they ate while everything was piping hot. Now the family sat around, lazy and sated.

Shaz brushed his fingertips over Camilla's bare arm. "You all right, baby girl?"

Her smile was serene, but there was something hidden behind her shuttered eyes. "I'm fine. Same as I was when you asked five minutes ago."

"That's not nice." Shaz assumed a wounded expression. "I'm simply concerned about your welfare."

A mischievous grin curved Camilla's lips and her eyes lit up. "My welfare and I are just fine."

He clasped her hand in his and kissed the back of it. They sat under an elm tree in the backyard, where Shaz was almost lulled into sleep by the ever-present breeze. His belly was full and he was content with Camilla next to him.

Teddy Bostwick had worked his usual magic with the grill. The succulent chicken and pork had been seasoned just right and enhanced by Paula's magic rub. Even now, the fragrant smoke drifted his way.

Roman, in typical fashion, arrived minutes ago with his family—a full hour after he should have gotten to their parents' house. The introductions were made and Paula prepared a plate for him and his wife, Venetia. Paula sat with their children—Dominic, who was six, and Shay, two-and-a-half years—trying to get them to eat. Ayanna had wandered over to them and Paula fed her from the same plate. Roman and Niecey sat a few feet away, teasing Shaz as they ate.

"Seems like we came at the right time," Roman said.

"You're right about that," Shaz shot back. "If you came any later, I'd have been on my second round."

"I doubt that," Niecey, chipped in. "Looks like you're too full to move." Her bright eyes danced as she laid the plate on her lap and twisted her long braids into a coil at the back of her neck.

Laughing, Shaz said, "That's the truth. I couldn't hold a message more, even if you whispered it."

After letting out a hearty burst of laughter, his father walked over with a fork in hand. "We still have lots left. May the best man eat his fill."

"Don't worry, I brought a container," Denise called from where she sat on an outdoor rocking chair with her eyes closed.

"Welcome to Bostwick Drive Through," Paula said, using one hand as a bullhorn. "Where guests come equipped with their own Tupperware."

Laughing, Denise said, "There's no way you and Daddy are gonna eat all that leftover food anyway. Trust me, I'm not feeling the least bit guilty about sucking up all your food, plus carting some away with me."

"I'd never make the mistake of thinking any such thing," Paula said, with a sweet smile.

The entire family laughed at her comment. As their amusement wound down, Martin and Sondra walked through the back door. "I'm empty and ready to fill up," Martin said, with his arm thrown around his wife's waist.

"Hey, everybody." Sondra waved at the group.

The family greeted them while Sondra moved toward two empty chairs. "Who's this little cutie?" she asked, as Ayanna toddled toward Sondra's open hands to investigate.

Shaz introduced Camilla and Sondra, and the two women exchanged greetings, then focused on Ayanna who chatted up Sondra in her own language. As she ran to her mother, Sondra's gaze followed her. When she looked up and caught Shaz watching her, Sondra's expression went from pensive to happy. But there were shadows in her eyes.

In his mind, he cursed his brother for being a selfish clod. Some things, Shaz was at liberty to say. Others, not so much. He figured his brother's continued refusal to have children was mired in his resentment of his father and their history. Why he brought that into his marriage, Shaz had no idea. In his career, sadly, he'd seen what unforgiveness and holding on to baggage from the past did to people. Too bad, Martin hadn't grown up enough to leave his bitterness behind.

As he crossed the grass with two plates, Martin watched his wife and the direction of her gaze. When his steps faltered, Shaz bit back a smile. Good for him. It was about time Martin thought about someone other than himself. Things would get ugly in his marriage if he hadn't told Sondra about his reluctance to have children, before they wed. Only God could help him if that was the case.

In the background, his father's music streamed from the house. All of them were used to Teddy Bostwick's love for 'the taste of Jamaica' as he called it. Now, Barrington Levy's *Too Experienced* wound his unique sound around the group as they engaged in small talk. When all the plates and utensils were collected, Paula stood and clapped her hands. Shaz immediately understood they were almost at the destination they'd been headed to since everybody arrived.

"Ladies, let's move to the kitchen," Paula announced.

"When's dessert?" Roman groused.

"When *I* say you can have it." Paula swept past them, with Shay in her arms and Dominic's hands in hers.

"After all these years, you still don't know your Mama." Teddy Bostwick chuckled as he took the seat Paula vacated. When the smile left his face, he added, "I need you all to come a little closer."

As soon as they settled in a loose circle around him, Teddy looked them each in the eyes in turn. "Nothing was settled after our meeting a couple of weeks ago. Your mama and I aren't gonna wait forever until you get yourselves sorted out."

Shaz knew his father had to be talking to his two older brothers because Shaz was a silent partner in the family business. After their father's revelation, Martin swore up and down that he wouldn't be running the business. This, despite the fact that he was most suited to do so.

Roman was already in the business in his role as an architect and vice president. But, Martin had a degree in business administration and a good head for business. He was simply mule-headed and unforgiving. If the business was to continue to thrive, that had to end now.

"What's preventing you from giving up your job at that firm and working for your family?" Shaz asked. "Although we already know what seventy-five percent of your answer's going to be."

Martin threw Shaz a silent, but deadly, gaze. After staring at his hands as if they held the key to the meaning of life, he still didn't answer.

Their father sighed, but before he spoke Roman butted in. "If you're afraid you won't be successful in the role, I'll—"

"I'm not afraid of anyone or anything." Martin's answer was much more vehement than it needed to be. He pursed his lips, then continued, "I just have other plans, that's all."

Shaz sucked his teeth and sat back. "You don't have any plans. You're simply doing this to get back at Mom and Dad because they need you."

Even the wind seemed to stop as Shaz spat his annoyance at his brother. Then everybody spoke at once, their tone strident, their words garbled.

When he couldn't get a word in, Teddy yelled, "Silence. All of you."

His head swivelled toward Shaz. "You need to apologize to your brother."

"What? For speaking the truth? We all know he's—"

"If your brother says he has plans, then he has plans." Teddy let that sink in before he added, "Because no son of mine would be small-minded enough to do something to jeopardise the financial security and stability of this family. Further, none of you would be so cruel as to want us to continue working when our heart isn't in it anymore."

Teddy Bostwick sighed and rubbed the stubble on his chin. "Everything we've built is for the four of you. It would be a shame if you three let other people come in and reap what they haven't sowed."

Shaz wanted to pump his fist and throw his arms around his father, but he did neither. Teddy *Bostwick is smarter than all three of his sons combined.* Their father was giving Martin enough rope to either hang himself or create something with it.

As Martin's skin flushed, he lowered his gaze and focused on the grass between his feet.

After Shaz and Roman exchanged a glance, they watched their father who studied his oldest son. Shaz and Roman continued their silent communication for another few seconds. Then, in an unspoken agreement, they got up and left Teddy and Martin to talk.

On the way to the kitchen, Roman looked sideways at Shaz. "You know, it's not too late to detour and come into the business."

"I'm not going there with you. You know that."

Roman stopped and faced him. "Dad had high hopes you'd say yes."

"Give it a rest. Construction isn't in my blood the way it is in yours or Martin's."

Arms folded, Martin said, "Try telling that to Dad."

Shaz's gaze met his father's, and with a slight shake of the head he let the older man know he wasn't up to the task. He'd have been blind or in denial not to admit the disappointment in his father's eyes was obvious. He sighed and tipped his head back. "It isn't right for me. Plus, I know nothing about the business."

"That's not true. You forget we all had to work for Dad during the summer. Even Denise."

"That's in the past and like I said—"

"You're not interested. I get it."

Eyes narrowed, Shaz stared Roman down. "You're not going to guilt me into giving up my life's work."

"Your *life's work* should include what you do for your family." He pointed to where Dad and Martin sat. "If he doesn't decide to get his act together, I'll be doing the work intended for three people."

"Don't start with the melodrama. We both know you're more capable than most people I know."

"That aside, the business needs you. How would you feel knowing Mom and Dad won't be able to retire because both you and Martin are playing hardball?"

"I'm not—"

"Suit yourself." Disgust was etched on Roman's face before he turned away and walked into the kitchen.

Shaz sighed and stared after him. Roman meant well and was fiercely loyal to family. He'd taken punishment for Shaz and intercepted school bullies many times when they were boys—up to the point where Shaz gained a few inches in height and worked on bulking up in the gym. Grateful or not, Shaz didn't intend to sacrifice his vision to build a family empire that would put money in his pockets but didn't bring him joy.

CHAPTER 18

Nothing Shaz heard at today's meeting comforted him. The Castle was rife with more misdeeds than they could sort out in a month or two. All the information he'd pieced together from what the other Kings provided, made him more concerned for Camilla.

Jai's voice pierced Shaz's mental cloud cover. "That completes my report on some approved meds and procedures by the State and my thoughts about how we can enhance the health facilities here."

"Sounds feasible," Vikkas said, to a rumble of agreement from the other men.

"You all right, Shaz?" Dro asked with a concerned expression. "You've hardly said a word."

"I'm good." He pulled his iPad closer. "I'm wrapping my head around some of the information you gathered over the weekend." He didn't speak to the other items weighing on his spirit.

A news item that turned his stomach had been seemingly linked to the adoption agency within The Castle. *Two-Year-Old Toddler Found Gutted In Dumpster*. In his research yesterday, he discovered the child was connected to an immigrant from Kenya who worked within The Castle walls. The baby had been a candidate for adoption with New Visions and had been placed with a family, who already had a child of the same age. Their biological child needed a liver transplant. The family's explanation was that during the adoption process, they were unaware that they were pregnant. When they found out, they terminated the adoption arrangements. A week earlier, the child had gone missing from a day care center. Frantic, the mother had reported the matter to the police. Days later, the toddler turned up in the dumpster. The weird thing was, the information trail tapered to a dead end. The file of the dead child had gone missing.

Shaz didn't want his mind to run any further on that track, but was willing to bet the liver the other child needed was harvested from the toddler found in the dumpster.

"With no further matters to be discussed, this meeting is terminated," Vikkas announced. "We reconvene next Monday."

Shaz didn't stick around to hear anything else. The most important matter had been first on the agenda—the updates on the attempted assassination of their mentor. Progress was slow and steady, but Shaz suspected that undertaking was bigger than it first appeared—the way the bulk of a glacier stayed hidden from the naked eye.

The culprits had plotted and executed their attack in such a way that there didn't seem to be a coordinated effort. The Kings were convinced nothing was further from the truth. Shaz was convinced time would reveal all the players involved in the assassination attempt.

He was deep in thought when Dwayne fell into step beside him as they headed for the elevator that would take them to the ground floor.

"Where are you off to in such a hurry?" Dwayne asked.

"I could ask you that," Shaz replied with a slight smirk.

"Educators always have minds waiting to be molded," Dwayne said, with his lips twitching.

"And lawyers are always one phone call away from a desperate client." The elevator arrived and as they stepped in, Shaz added, "I'm headed to the Information & Systems department. I did want to throw you an invite though."

"Let me hear it," Dwayne said, looking sideways at Shaz.

"My colleague and I run an activity centre for boys between the age of twelve and nineteen. We've developed what we called the Evanston

Gentlemen's Club. What we do is try and teach them social and life skills so they can function in various situations. I'd like you to come in and give them a motivational talk. At your convenience, of course."

"Consider it done," Dwayne said. "I'll come back to you with some dates."

"Appreciate it." Shaz held out his hand to Dwayne.

After staring at it for several seconds, Dwayne ignored his hand and pulled him into a one shoulder hug.

They parted ways on the ground floor and Shaz went deeper into the building to find the IS Department. The electronic directory he carried via his phone led him through various levels of security to a one-story building connected to the main building by a covered walkway.

The passkey he'd been issued gave him access to all the administrative units with the Castle. The only place he didn't have free access to was the lab facility where Daron created all the genius geek-technology that kept the Kings safe and functioning in their diverse operational capacities.

A heavy glass door led into a reception area with white ceramic tiles, walls, and fluorescent lighting that reminded him more of a medical facility than an information hive.

The thin, strawberry blond woman behind a secretary's desk stood when he entered. "Mr. Bostwick, good day."

"Same to you, Cyndi," he said, reading from her name tag.

"What can I do for you today?" Cyndi's smile and words were pleasant.

"I'll be using the library and the retrieval system." He pointed toward a frosted glass door. "I'll see myself inside."

Her response didn't come immediately, then she caught herself. "Not a problem, sir."

Shaz figured she'd never witnessed a director doing any research for himself. Her wide eyes had given away her surprise. No doubt, he'd be the subject of conversation between Cyndi and her colleagues.

He frowned when his memory failed him. "How many people work in this department?"

"Only ten of us, sir."

"Thanks. I'll call if I need you."

Shaz went around the corner and into a corridor with three doors on each side. According to the layout, they were offices. The end of the corridor opened into a huge library with a massive circular table, similar to the one in the board room. This table was a solid block of wood surrounded by executive chairs and drop-down lights that hovered above each seat. Three walls were lined with floor-to-ceiling file cabinets. The other wall had a sheet of wood that matched the table top. He guessed it hid a screen.

As far as Shaz knew, all the businesses housed on Castle property had information stored on the central server. Remote access hadn't been a problem for him. He needed to get his hands on actual files. Cutting out the middle man meant nobody would have a record of what files he'd been studying. Unless, there were cameras installed. Shaz had no doubt about that. He scanned the lights and the ceiling, wondering who was viewing those cameras. Until he was sure Daron had a handle on who was watching what, he'd stay out of the range of any hidden devices. A look inside the one door in the room led him to rows of shelving with empty storage boxes and step ladders at several heights.

After circling the room once to understand the layout of the filing system, he removed his jacket. Masking a chuckle, he made another circuit, pulling out several files as he went. Then, he examined the documents in each file changing position every so often, even to the extent of perching on a step ladder in the storage closet.

He couldn't help noticing that some information he expected to be in several files was missing. That small inconvenience didn't bother him. All the files had electronic copies and those weren't as easy to tamper with. Daron had done a thorough job of converting every shred of data in the first month of their appointment to the board. He created two sets of e-files. One for the Castle and another, now stored in a secure data bank, accessible only to the Kings of the Castle.

Verifying the paper trail he needed took Shaz an hour, after which he replaced all the files he removed, except for one. That was a tester. As he went past the blonde, she cleared her throat and stood. "Um, Mr. Bostwick?"

Shaz produced his most charming smile. "Yes?"

"Um. Nobody is allowed to remove files from the library."

He faced Cyndi full on. Tipping one brow, he said, "Not even directors?"

With a wary smile in place, she moved her head side to side. "Regulations."

"Made by whom?"

Cyndi's smile faded. "The previous board, sir."

"New board. New rules." He laid the file on the desk and slid both hands into his pockets. "I hope you were as stringent with the last set of directors."

A pink tide flooded her face and she stuttered. "I-I'm sorry, sir."

He held up both hands. "It's okay. Since the new regulations haven't filtered down, I'll leave the file with you."

She picked it up and brushed aside the hair on her forehead. A few strands stuck to her skin and she swiped her forehead. "T-thanks for your understanding."

"Not a problem, Cyndi."

Deliberately, Daron hadn't been in a rush to shake up the Information & Systems department. He had a bead on their activities and didn't want them ruffled while he did those infamous technical gymnastics in the background.

Shaz felt Cyndi's gaze as he walked out the door. From her reaction, he figured that someone would be interested in that particular file. Whoever that was would be sure to come knocking down Shaz's door.

CHAPTER 19

Camilla turned wide eyes on Shaz. She lifted the gift box in her hand. "You know I can't accept these, right?"

With an arm around her shoulder, Shaz pulled Camilla closer and nuzzled her neck. "No, I don't know any such thing. I've never given you anything, so—"

"And you want to start with something this expensive?" She pulled away to look at him. "If you're starting at diamond level, where are you gonna go from there?"

"Don't worry about it, that's for me to think about."

Camilla scooted forward on the sofa. "Ayanna, don't touch that."

She got up and moved Shaz's iPad to the shelving across the room and handed him his phone. "In my situation, I don't want to have to replace any luxury items."

With an easy grin, he pulled her back to the sofa, then held out one hand to Ayanna. "Come, baby girl."

She ran into his arms and giggled when Shaz lifted her over his head, then placed her on his lap. "How much longer d'you have to wait before she comes up for treatment?"

Camilla's gaze turned pensive. "Another week or two, depending on what happens with the waiting list."

"Your visa. That's important. After she has the procedure, there's the recovery time and you don't want to have any issues."

Massaging the back of her neck, Camilla met his eyes. "I know. I wasn't getting anywhere with the Jamaican High Commission here, so I'm going to have to do an emergency interview back on the island."

"When's your appointment?"

She lowered her gaze, looking shamefaced. "I haven't fixed it yet."

He slid his arm around Camilla while Ayanna climbed from his lap to hers. "Baby girl, you can't put this off. Already you've wasted too much time."

Laying her head against his shoulder, she sighed. "I know. I'll do it tomorrow. I promise."

After dropping a soft kiss on her forehead, Shaz whispered, "Don't delay, just do it."

Eyes closed, she nodded. "I will."

He lifted her hand that was wrapped around the box with the earrings. "Do me a favor and try them on."

Her forehead wrinkled as she studied the box. "Are you trying to trick me into wearing them?"

"Yes and no," he said, deciding to come clean. Somewhat.

Camilla leaned away from him. "What does that mean?"

He weighed the merits to her wearing the earrings against going without them and made up his mind to tell her everything. "This is the deal," he said. In two minutes, he explained why it was important for her to put in the earrings.

She mulled over the information, staring at the blank television screen. Seconds later, she picked up the remote and found a channel showing cartoons. Then she set Ayanna on the floor. The little girl stood in front of the center table, her eyes glued to the set.

"When you put it like that," Camilla said, her tone sober. "It's hard to refuse your offer."

Shocked at the ease with which she gave in, Shaz slid the box out of her hands and opened it.

With her lip caught between her teeth, she removed the earrings from the ear nuts and put them in. "Thank you," she said softly. "I just can't lose Ayanna. I would die if anything happened to her."

"I know, hon." He was pleased she'd listened to reason but now wasn't the time to say the earrings looked good on her.

"Come here, baby." Camilla lifted Ayanna, who protested over the interruption between her and the television set. "It's okay, just let me put these in."

Aside from touching her ears as Camilla removed the pair of knobs she wore, Ayanna didn't fuss.

"Thanks." Shaz ruffled her hair. "That's one less thing to worry about."

After releasing Ayanna, Camilla angled her body toward Shaz. "I do have one question."

"What's are these? You in a lodge or something?"

She lifted his hands and ran her thumb over the imprint of a lion's head enclosed in three circles. Nine spearheads completed the artistry on the inside of his wrists.

"That's two questions." Shaz took her hand in his. "And no, I'm not in a lodge. This artwork is a symbol of the work I do and my connection to the other Kings of The Castle."

Camilla threw him a doubtful look, then repositioned his hand to study one of the tattoos. "The detail is amazing. It looks cultish and meaningful."

"You sound like a conspiracy theorist," he said, chuckling. "If you ever need one, I can link you with the artist."

She glanced at Ayanna, then said, "I'll be sure to let you know if I ever feel the need."

With one arm around Camilla, Shaz kissed the side of her forehead. What he couldn't disclose about the tattoos was that they were part of Daron's genius. In the event that Shaz was ever kidnapped, by pressing his wrists together he'd activate a tracking device that would reveal his location. He'd been forced to give away the true function of the earrings to secure Camilla's cooperation. The tattoos, she didn't need to know or worry about.

A car pulled up at the sidewalk and a door slammed.

Shaz glanced at the time, assuming Miss Mabel had arrived home, but she didn't appear. Roughly five minutes later, she let herself in. Her bright smile rivaled the light bulb in the ceiling. "Glad ya still here, Shaz. I notice you never come today, so I bring home the roast beef you asked me to save for you."

"I got busy around lunchtime and forgot to get it."

"Dat's why ya so skinny. Anyway, ya not di only one." She pointed toward the street. "The young man in the car look like him could use some more flesh on his bones, so I brought him something, too."

Miss Mabel bustled past them toward the kitchen with Ayanna dogging her footsteps.

"Your auntie is something else. She'd feed the whole nation, if possible." He chuckled as he picked up his food where Miss Mabel left it on the table. With his other hand, he pulled Camilla to her feet. "Time to head home."

Camilla sent him a mock glare. "You just want to be alone with all that good food."

Laughing, Shaz conceded, "I cannot deny the truth."

A sweet kiss in the doorway made him regret that they'd be separated until Wednesday, when he saw her again. He was about to tell her when Ayanna tottered into the room and waved at him. "Bye, Sha."

Waving back at her, he said goodbye and blew her a kiss.

She put a hand to her mouth and tried to imitate his action, which had him and Camilla chuckling.

In the Alfa Romeo, Shaz mentally scrolled through what he'd found out at The Castle's data bank. He'd spent the afternoon connecting dots between what he saw as related cases. Meantime, he'd let the information marinate in his mind, until it all gelled together in an orderly and cohesive way. Then he'd lock in on his targets.

His ride home was uneventful and he ate a few mouthfuls of the roast beef before putting the container in the refrigerator. After a long shower and falling into bed, he picked up the remote and switched on the 75" television tethered to the wall. He chose a news magazine programme to watch while reading the documents downloaded to his iPad. At ten-thirty, he put aside the iPad and switched off the light.

As he cleared his mind, he thought how different things would be if Camilla agreed to move in. He wouldn't have to worry. The security detail would become unnecessary. Ayanna was a sweet little addition to the deal. She was a quick learner and amusing when she tried saying his words back to him. He wasn't saying he was anywhere close to wanting to propose. They both had so much more to learn about each other, but Camilla made him want to do things differently since she walked into his life. The woman had taken him by storm, trying to make him work harder and faster than he planned on her behalf. He could definitely see her in his future.

At first, Shaz wasn't sure what woke him. The television was still on and a rerun of an earlier news magazine programme was in progress. The soft pulsing of his phone alerted him. He was pretty sure it wasn't time to get up. He picked up the cellular, looked at the display, and every nerve in his body stood on end. "Camilla, what's wrong?"

"It's me, Mabel." Her pitch was way outside her normal range, considering that she always spoke at the top of her lungs.

Jack-knifing to a sitting position, Shaz lowered the sound on the television. "Slow down and say that again, Miss Mabel."

"Boy, open ya ears nuh man." He ignored the insult and waited for her to go on. "Some men just came to the house, told Camilla to dress. They took the baby, too. I'm in the car with ya security following dem."

"Where are they headed?" he asked, striding to the closet.

"How me fi know? Maybe downtown." Miss Mabel's voice quivered, unnerving Shaz. "We seem to be driving in circles though. Only God knows where we goin'."

Shaz lowered his pitch. "Let me speak with Daniel, please."

"Good night, Shaz. What Miss Mabel says is true." Daniel's crisp tone was reassuring. Still, Shaz didn't breathe. "They seem to be driving in ever-widening circles. Why, I don't know."

"I think I know the reason." Shaz moved the phone from his ear as he pulled on a shirt. "Stay with them. I'll call you back in a few."

Shaz stepped into his pants and shoved his feet into the first pair of shoes he found. When he sat in his car, he got Daniel on the line. "Where are you now and where are Camilla and Ayanna?"

Daniel gave him their location, which was the police station. That was weird. If she'd been picked up for possible deportation, she'd have been taken to a detention facility.

"I'll meet you there in ten."

On arrival, Shaz stalked into the building and addressed the duty officer. "I'm Shastra Bostwick. You're holding Miss Camilla Gibson, who was brought here some minutes ago. I'm her lawyer and I'd like to see her."

"Give me a minute," the balding officer said, lowering his gaze to a log book.

Without apology or a blip on his conscience, Shaz went from mild-mannered to difficult with no stops in between. He tapped the counter with the flat of his hand. "No, I'm going to need you to deal with this now. My client wasn't given the courtesy of knowing why she was being detained when the officers took her from her home."

Camilla might have been skirting close to violating the six-month time limit she had in America, but she still had a few days left before she'd be outside the law.

"Sir, I'm going to—"

With his voice at a level he never used, Shaz said, "And *I'm* going to need you to act on the double. I need to see my client in the next few minutes, especially since—to the best of my knowledge—she hasn't been charged with anything."

"But sir—"

"If that doesn't happen." Shaz folded his arms and stood with his legs spread apart. "I'm not only going to sue the governor of the State, I'll extend that to the local civic authorities, this police department, plus the officers involved in Camilla's detention." He pointed to the policeman. "And you, so please ensure that I speak with your commanding officer. Now."

The man raced away as if a host of demons from hell were hot on his heels.

Miss Mabel hovered at his elbow, but when his gaze landed on her, she shrank back as if afraid his fury would extend to her, too.

He quirked one side of his mouth and murmured to her to have a seat.

In return, she bobbed her head in a slight nod, then went to do as he suggested.

While he waited, Shaz prowled the space like a hungry leopard who'd caught wind of its prey. The commanding officer was a hefty, personable man, who understood that Shaz would not be deterred. "Give us a few more minutes to get Miss Gibson's things and have her released," he said, after they spoke. "My apologies for this inconvenience—"

"That never should have happened, but I don't suppose I'll get an explanation for this foolishness since no one has accused my client of a crime."

He avoided Shaz's gaze while a maroon tide crept upward on his neck. He turned away. Almost stumbling over his feet in his haste. "I'll be right back."

The entire ordeal took an interminable forty-five minutes before Camilla appeared.

As she walked toward him, hugging herself, his scalp prickled. Camilla's wide eyes intensified the fear crawling in his gut. He knew exactly what it meant to have his stomach plummet to his feet. He gripped her by both arms as she whisked away her tears with the back of one hand. Before she spoke, he anticipated the words that were a like a blow to the solar plexus.

"They took my baby, Shaz," she cried. "Where's Ayanna?"

CHAPTER 20

This was the longest night of Shaz's life.

Camilla's earlier story still tore at his gut. When she realized Ayanna had been loaded into a separate vehicle, she tried calling Aunt Mabel but wasn't allowed to use the phone. The first thing the officers did was confiscate it.

Her face was ravaged—eyes red, features swollen from the tears she shed. Meanwhile, Shaz was at his wits' end trying to figure out where the police, and whoever else was behind that bit of skullduggery, had hidden the little girl. A total information blackout faced them. As best as Miss Mabel recalled, three units were parked outside the house. Two police cars and one unmarked vehicle.

Daniel backed up that story and earned Shaz's eternal gratitude by getting the license plate numbers as the convoy drove away from the house. The challenge was, the number on the unmarked car led nowhere—almost as if it had been given phony plates. Frustration bubbled inside him when Daron conveyed this information. Shaz racked his mind to figure out the next logical step.

When Dro and Reno met him at Miss Mabel's house, he insisted on going with them to find Ayanna. Only the Lord knew how Camilla had the presence of mind to activate the earrings when she first left the house. With the tracking device engaged, Daron was able to tell him, via phone, that Ayanna was stationary and that he had members of his team watching the location—a house, ten minutes away, in Chicago. Daron was on his way there.

Dro, Reno, and Shaz stood together on the verandah strategizing, while Camilla walked aimlessly around the living room.

"I'm coming with you," Shaz said, as the other two men prepared to leave.

"Are you sure that's the right thing to do?" Dro asked, lifting his chin toward the house. "Looks to me like Camilla needs you."

Shaz glanced over his shoulder and rubbed his jaw. "With the security in place Camilla and Miss Mabel will be fine."

"He's right," Reno insisted, "Your place is with her. Let us do this. We'll keep you updated and that way, the two of you will know what's going on."

After a tense moment of silence, Shaz let out his breath and grumbled. "That makes sense but keep me in the loop every step of the way."

"You've got it," Dro said, resting a hand on his shoulder.

As both men left the verandah, Shaz entered the living room. He went straight to Camilla, whose eyes reflected her desperation and wrapped his arms around her. "The team will do everything they can. I know it's hard, but keep your chin up. You did good activating the earrings. That will ensure they bring Ayanna back. Trust me on that, okay?"

She nodded, then pressed her face against his chest. Her warm tears soaked his shirt.

As she cried, Shaz stroked her hair and whispered comforting words. Gently, he pressed kisses to her forehead and hair. When she stopped crying, he urged her to wash her face.

Camilla didn't look any better after she returned, and at that point more words would have been trite. Her obvious pain twisted his gut and made him feel useless.

The minutes dragged, coagulated into one hour, then two. Daron sent a text advising that Ayanna and her captors were on the move.

Meantime, Camilla and Miss Mabel were inconsolable. The two of them sat staring at the blank television screen as if someone had died. Shaz stalked back and forth, checking his phone every few minutes.

Hope lit Camilla's eyes, then faded each time Shaz suppressed whatever update Daron provided. After each instance, he died a little inside.

At two o'clock when the police could provide no information and didn't seem inclined to right the wrong that came through their foul-up or collusion, Shaz dragged a hand over his face. Only God knew where they'd be without the Kings doing their part.

Camilla's soft sobs, then her catatonic behavior did a number on his nerves. Shaz was as helpless as a newborn baby and he hated it. Nothing fazed, weakened, or overcame him. Now, a woman and a baby he'd grown to love did all that. In one blow. He rubbed both sides of his jaw, weighed down by the hopelessness in Camilla's eyes.

He suspected there were several things at work, but come the morning he'd start uprooting things inside The Castle with a vengeance. Shaz knew how to play in the light and he also knew how to skate close to the darkness. This game had turned dirty and it was time to respond the way his opponents would understand. Office hours were but a few hours away. Waiting was also a strategy. He wanted those who were behind this cruel act to know he was on their trail.

His phone pulsed and he looked at the screen.

Dro had sent him a text. *Closing in on new location. Ayanna stationary. Stand by.*

For the next fifteen minutes, Shaz paced the area around the sofa. The cadence of his heartbeat was fast and heavy. Containing his excitement was hard, but Shaz managed not to give away anything. He'd wait until Daron confirmed that Ayanna was safe before he told Camilla.

Those earrings were a godsend. He sent up thanks and prayed Ayanna hadn't been harmed. He had his doubts anybody would touch her, if the Alderman had anything to do with this show of power.

Another text lit his phone display. *On location. Getting ready to move.*

Shaz looked up from the cell and Camilla's gaze sharpened. "You heard something?"

"Give it time," he said, sickened that he had to watch her succumb to despair once more. "I'll tell you when I have news."

The atmosphere was like that of a mausoleum, but he stuffed both hands into his pockets and stayed on his feet as his mind wrapped around what might be happening with his fellow Kings.

"Shaz?" Camilla pressed a hand to her forehead and pulled in a deep breath. "D'you really think they'll bring her home?"

He nodded, wanting to hug her until her fears slipped away. "Daron, Dro, and Reno are good at what they do. We just need to give them time."

Miss Mabel's head drooped and she jerked awake. She yawned, rubbed her eyes and was nodding off again, when Camilla spoke softly, "Auntie, it doesn't make sense for you to lose your sleep, too. You should go lie down."

Miss Mabel shook her head. "I wouldn't feel good to be sleeping when I don't know where my grandniece is and what might be happening to her."

With a faint smile, Camilla reassured her aunt. "You have to be at work in the morning, so I'll call you when we hear something. Promise."

"Make sure." Miss Mabel eased to her feet, stretching as she did. "I'm not as young as I used to be. Can't keep up."

Normally, her comments amused Shaz. This time, all he could muster was a faint smile. He was on edge, but held his composure. Camilla and he waited for another twenty minutes before another text came through. This time from Daron. *Mission complete.*

That's when he told Camilla that Ayanna was coming home. She unravelled, sobbing in his arms while he dropped soft kisses on her temple. "Don't cry, hon. It's almost over."

Camilla refused to sit still after that, and rushed to the door at every hum of an engine.

Dawn was approaching when a vehicle drew up outside Miss Mabel's house.

Shaz strode to the door and yanked it open. Daron, dressed in what looked like black combat gear, opened the front passenger door of a black Ram ProMaster cargo van. Reno, who wore similar garb, also got out of the vehicle. From the back seat, Daron lifted a swaddled bundle from Dro's arms and stood straight.

Before Shaz could get a word out, or move a muscle, Camilla shot past him and ran straight at Daron. She lifted Ayanna from his arms and squeezed the sleeping toddler to her chest while tears streamed from her puffy eyes.

"Thank you," Camilla whispered repeatedly as she opened the blanket and did a tactile and visual scan.

Daron saluted her as she turned toward the house. Dro and Reno stood aside and allowed her to pass. The early morning chill and an unnatural silence settled around them as Camilla disappeared inside the house. When the door closed behind her, Daron faced Shaz, pulled out his phone and scrolled to a photo. "Do you know this guy?"

Shaz pinched the photo and opened it up on the screen. The guy in the picture was the same one who'd been watching him outside the gym. He still hadn't figured out why he seemed so familiar.

Frowning, Shaz asked, "Who's he, really?"

"A small-time con artist. Has a record for small stuff. This time though, he won't get off so easy."

"I'm assuming you have him in lockup?"

"Put it this way." He glanced at Dro and Reno. "We have him on lockdown while he thinks about who he's gonna give up to gain some time off his sentence."

Shaz knew not to ask where he was being kept or who else made up that *we*. Instead, he went in another direction. "Was he the one driving the car?"

Daron and Dro exchanged a glance, then he eyeballed Shaz. The tilt of Daron's head and his folded arms told Shaz he was asking too many questions. With a weary smile, he conceded. "Scratch that. I don't need to know."

After a sharp nod of approval and another silent exchange with Dro, Daron turned away.

"One last thing." Shaz stopped him by grabbing his arm. "Those earrings. They're a brilliant touch ... and to think we figured they were over the top when you first introduced them as a security measure. Can't thank you enough."

A wry smile came to Daron's lips. "Yes, my gadgets deserve respect, but you're more than welcome."

"Yeah. Talk later." Shaz set his jaw, then gritted out, "I'll be rattling some cages, starting today."

"The woman and the baby inside are definitely worth it. Do what you have to," Daron said as he went down the front steps.

"You best believe I will." Shaz included Dro and Reno as they went past him. "Thanks for everything."

Daron grinned. "You need to stop thanking us for carrying out our obligations. One for all and all that jazz …"

"That's right." Dro and Reno laughed because they both spoke the same words.

Hands in his pockets, Shaz watched as the vehicle rolled away. He looked up as fingers of daylight traced across the sky and offered up a prayer of thanks. The baby was back, and Camilla was happy. That meant he, too, was content.

Last night had brought him to a turning point. His woman's agony turned him inside out and changed something in him. He wanted, no *needed*, Camilla in his life. He wanted to love, protect, and keep her safe from anything that could harm her or Ayanna.

Still, he was facing the most important battle of his life. The critical thing was, he had the influence and the network he needed to strike a blow against those Khalil was trying to eject from The Castle and restore its former reputation. The fact that these issues were intersecting meant he had to stay vigilant until he and the Kings brought everything to a satisfactory close.

CHAPTER 21

Shaz folded his hands on the desk and wore a confident smile. He needed sleep after the stress of last night, but that had to go on a backburner. To Georgiana, he said, "I'm sorry to call you in at such short notice, but I need your help."

The teenager threw her mother a fleeting look and sank lower in the visitor's chair.

"Georgiana," he said to get her attention. "There's no need to be afraid. Have you heard from Hussey since you were here last time?"

She shook her head.

Soraya chided her. "I didn't raise a dummy. Answer when Mr. Bostwick talks to you."

"No." Georgiana raised her chin. "He ain't bothered me since then." She frowned, then glanced at her mother, before throwing an accusation his way. "Nicole didn't come back."

"We're working on it and that's why I need your help."

Despite discreet inquiries and analyzing footage from security cameras, The Hub remained an impenetrable fortress. For now, Shaz reminded himself.

"What you wanna know?" Georgiana asked, her eyes glinting with suspicion.

He included Soraya in his carefully worded statement. "I could lie to you and tell you I'm only trying to find Nicole, but since there are other persons involved, we'd like to help them, too. You get me?"

She nodded and her brows cleared.

He picked up a pen and pulled a notepad in front of him. "I want you to tell me everything you remember about The Castle. Where you were kept. How many other girls were around you. Who took care of all of you—"

"I was only in there for a month, so I—"

Shaz held up both hands to reassure her. "That's okay. Whatever you remember will help me."

After clasping her mother's hand, Georgiana closed her eyes and relayed her experience from memory. At one point, she scrubbed her eyes with the heels of her hand and sniffled. Then her eyes popped open. "Water."

With his head cocked toward her, Shaz waited.

Georgiana sat forward, and her voice rang with excitement. "Late at nights, we could hear the sound of water. I dunno if it was a river or a waterfall or what, but when it got real late and we were quiet, we heard it."

One side of Shaz's mouth tipped up as his heart accelerated. That bit of information put him closer to finding the place where the girls were being kept.

A sad note crept into Georgiana's voice as she continued, "I heard there were pregnant girls there, too, but I never saw them … we heard stories about the babies."

"Like what?" His pen poised over the paper while he held Georgiana's gaze.

She used her knuckles to dry a line of tears. "That they were taken away as soon as they were born and sold to rich people."

"Were there only Black girls, Georgiana?"

Slowly she moved her head side to side. "No. A mixture. Chinese. Indian. White. Some from the islands."

With both hands thrust in his pockets, Shaz paced the room, staring at his shoes while absorbing what he'd been told. He moved toward the potted plant next to the window, simply because he didn't want Georgiana and Saroya to see the effect the story had on him. They were from the surrounding neighborhoods, so the same thing could easily have happened to his sister. Snatched as she went about her business and put into sexual slavery or forced to produce a baby for twisted people who chose to take advantage of the poor.

When he returned to the desk, he clasped both hands in front of him. "In the event that we have to go to court, can I count on you to testify?"

She shot a panicked look at her mother, who gripped her hand. "Think about all the other girls you'll be helping."

Her shoulders heaved and she lowered her head. As her breathing evened out, she swallowed hard and looked at him. "Yeah, you said Hussey wouldn't come back and he ain't bothered me, so I know I can trust you."

The breath Shaz wasn't aware he was holding seeped out of him. "Thank you. Remember this, when you know what you want to do in the future, come and talk to me. Not everything inside The Castle is bad, as I'm sure you know. We want to help people, too. That's why the place was originally set up. To facilitate people living their dreams."

Georgiana exchanged an excited smile with her mother, who blinked back tears. "Thank you," she whispered.

"It's the least I can do." His gaze went back to Georgiana. "I'm going to ask you not to discuss what we've talked about with anyone. When we get those girls out, you'll know. I promise."

Both females thanked him. At the doorway, Georgiana offered him a shy smile, while her mother nodded as if she knew something he didn't. Then she said, "It's true what they say about you on the street. You may be a bigshot, but you look out for the poor."

Humbled, Shaz simply nodded once. Their obvious gratitude did a number on him and he couldn't come up with any words.

* * *

Twice in one day, Shaz was dumbstruck. First, because of his encounter with Soraya and Georgiana. Now, Camilla's cool acceptance of his request to have a serious talk with her knocked him sideways. He was used to her protesting before he stated what he wanted her to do.

He removed his tie and hung it over his knee.

Ayanna, who was occupied with a pack of colorful flashcards on the other side of the center table made a beeline for him. Babbling, she grabbed the tie and hung it over her shoulders.

"Come, baby." Camilla beckoned to her and attempted to get the tie.

While Ayanna fussed, Camilla lifted her onto the sofa between them and kept a hold on the tie. "It's not safe for you to play with this, boo-boo."

That didn't stop Ayanna from pulling the blue silk material through her hands.

Camilla watched him over Ayanna's head as if preparing herself for the worst. "What did you want to ask me?"

"I want to move you to The Castle. Today."

She looked at him sideways. "You're back with that again?"

Eyebrows raised, he asked, "After last night, did you expect anything else?"

Her focus went to Ayanna and she gently removed the tie from her mouth. "It's not for eating, baby."

When Camilla wouldn't look at him, Shaz outlined things the way they were. "On the grounds we have twenty-four-hour security, plus cameras. Until we sort everything out, I'd feel better if you stay with me. The place has two bedrooms, so there's no pressure."

Camilla smirked. "I didn't think you were hard up for sex."

Ayanna looked up. "Mommy. Sez?"

Holding back laughter, Camilla said, "Not quite, honey."

The moment she looked at Shaz, they both chuckled. As their amusement died, Camilla's expression was thoughtful. "What about Aunt Mabel?"

'She's a wise woman. Miss Mabel knows this is not about her." What he didn't add was that he'd already spoken to Miss Mabel, who gave him her blessing and told him she didn't need any security outside her door if Camilla chose to go to his place.

Shaz wasn't so sure. People with this level of tenacity had few boundaries when it came to getting what they wanted.

Running both hands through her hair, Camilla let out her breath. She stared at the flashcards before her attention came back to him. "Thank you. I think it would be easier on all of us if I accept your offer."

He masked his surprise and sent an affectionate smile her way. "Yes, that makes life much simpler."

As her brows crumpled, Camilla asked, "Are you sure Aunt Mabel will be safe?"

Though he knew the older woman would give him hell, he conceded to what he knew she didn't want. "We can leave the security in place here for a few more days, if that makes you feel better."

A brilliant smile replaced Camilla's frown. "It does."

She picked up Ayanna and kissed her cheek. "We're moving house, babes."

Turning her attention to Shaz, she asked, "Can you give me an hour or so to get our things together?"

He pulled out his iPad from where he stashed it in the corner of the sofa. "Sure. I'll get some stuff done while I wait."

Camilla edged closer to him and placed a soft kiss on his jaw. "Thank you."

Her warm breath caressed his skin and sent heat shooting through his lap. With the baby in her arms, he couldn't kiss her properly but there would be other times. "No problem. But there is one more thing."

"What's that?"

"We are going to make that emergency appointment for a U.S. embassy visit."

Camilla didn't seem convinced, so while Ayanna muttered to herself, he squeezed her mother's arm. Their eyes connected. "You can't keep putting it off. We're doing it this evening."

In a small voice, she said, "Okay. With everything going haywire, I didn't get around to it."

Although from here on in they would be playing house, Shaz was invested in keeping Camilla and Ayanna out of sight while he unraveled the web of abuse and exploitation within The Castle.

CHAPTER 22

"If I had known you planned to blindside me, I wouldn't have answered my phone."

Roman chuckled. "I never give up as long as there's a chance I might win."

"Bro, you're fighting a losing battle." Shaz leaned against the wall outside the conference room at The Castle.

Vikkas had called them to an emergency meeting this afternoon at Daron's request. The information Georgiana gave Shaz provided the catalyst for the surveillance plan Daron put in motion. He and Dro preferred to watch the pattern of movement by their main targets—the Alderman and his lawyer—plus do their other technical fancy footwork, before making any moves. Plus, they had to scope out the property. A week later, something major was on the horizon.

Roman's impatient tone cut into Shaz's thoughts. "I just want you to think about the fact that aside from being disappointed, our parents will have to put off their trip."

"They've gone away before—"

"But not on an extended trip."

Shaz studied the shiny toes of his leather Oxfords. "And why are their movements your con—"

"They could do want they want, if you'd stop being selfish and do what Dad doesn't want to have to bow and scrape to have you do."

"What the heck did you just say? You must be—"

"You know exactly what I mean."

Suddenly irritated, Shaz snapped. "You're rude, you know that?"

"You're not the first person to say so."

Shaz paced the length of the wall as he ranted. "Every time we talk, I can't get a word in edgewise and when I finally do, you keep cutting me off. And by the way, I'm *not* selfish."

"Whatever, but I know whatever you're doing over there at The Castle isn't more important than our family business."

"Ugh." Shaz tipped his chin toward the ceiling and rubbed the back of his neck.

On his way into the boardroom, Dro tapped his watch and gave Shaz a meaningful look.

"Roman, I have to go." Shaz shoved a hand into his pocket, tangling his fingers with the medallion, which grounded him. "Despite what you think about what I'm doing here, it's just as important, more so in fact, than putting up buildings."

His brother's tone was grudging. "Only to an extent. People need places to raise their families. Bostwick Construction facilitates that."

"I don't have time to argue. Next time, miss me with the guilt trips and browbeating."

"This might be a joke to you but the company means everything to me." Roman's voice was heavy with disappointment, but Shaz wasn't moved.

"Which is why you should give me a break and think about running it yourself." Through his teeth Shaz ground out. "I have to go."

He fell in step with Grant and walked into the boardroom where the other Kings had gathered. As he sat at the circular table, Shaz's emotions ping-ponged between exasperation and contentment. Since Roman got on the phone, his mood took a downhill turn.

He was beyond satisfied that Camilla and Ayanna were settling into his suite, but his family was the limit. Roman had upped the ante and continued badgering him every few days, but they both knew Shaz was stubborn and wasn't likely to give in to pressure.

His attention settled on the men around him when Vikkas called the meeting to order. After introductory remarks in the space of two minutes, he went to the most pressing agenda item.

Daron took over by walking to the screen Vikkas had activated and tapping it to enlarge a building at one corner. "Based on information Shaz received, Dro and I have been able to connect many dots as it pertains to the layout within The Castle."

He pointed to the screen. "So, The Hub is here. There's an enclosed walkway behind that leads to another section of the building. If Shaz's client hadn't mentioned the water component, we'd never have thought of that artificial waterfall that's part of the ornamental garden."

Frowning, Daron continued, "When Grant and Reno compared the architectural drawings to the original I found, something didn't add up."

"How so?" Dwayne asked.

"With the mention of the waterfall, we had another look. We discovered that one of the previous directors had it installed." Daron pointed to Grant, then Reno. "The architects among us determined that an annex was built onto the original building that housed the adoption agency … without Khalil's knowledge or approval."

Kaleb let out a long whistle. "These guys aren't playing."

"And that is why we have to hit them hard, so they know this kind of crap is unacceptable," Shaz said, rubbing his jaw as he focused on the screen.

"Agreed," With one finger, Daron traced the walkway onscreen. "So, with the building reconfigured and secured this way, and the girls in close proximity, no one would ever know where they came from."

Daron swiped the screen to reveal another picture. This one showed small enclosures with single beds and shelving. Each cell contained a young woman. On the outside, a female security guard paced the corridor. "This unit, for want of a better term, is confined to one floor. On the other side is where they keep the young mothers."

This time, when the picture changed, the men gasped. The shot captured six cells. A pregnant woman occupied each. Daron faced them, hands in his pockets. "The only exit from this place is via a service entry close to the waterfall. The building is self-sufficient, so Shaz's client was really courageous and smart to use the opportunity to escape in that private ambulance."

Everyone in the room fell silent. Their facial expressions ranged from open disgust to outrage.

"Should I even ask why an ambulance was on the premises," Kaleb said, tapping his thumb in a slow beat on the surface of the table.

"From the footage we've managed to get, one of the girls took ill and had to be rushed to hospital," Daron replied.

"A private one, of course," Dro added. "Where clients pay premium fees and few questions are asked."

Shaz nodded, then frowned. "Wait. How did you two get inside to lay all these digital tracks, since The Hub has its own staff and what not?"

"This is where you have to be enterprising," Dro said, chuckling. "Although we have cause for concern as there seems to be a blackout area for which we don't have visuals."

Daron's slow smile signaled his agreement. "The place is self-sufficient, but the workers do go home on weekend breaks and days off. See, you pick your target carefully so that when you roll up to do some, uh, maintenance, you get ready access to the premises."

"We're not even going to ask how you got in and out," Jai said, peering at the screen.

"Right." Daron's mouth quirked in a slight smile.

"So the point of this meeting is to put all of us on high alert." Daron met each man's eyes for a second. "We're about to do a crash course on the layout. By the time we leave here, all of us will know exactly where every room, entrance and exit are in the Hub. We won't be providing you with copies of these slides. The less physical evidence we have, the less likely it is that what we're doing will reach the wrong eyes or ears."

"Are we ready?" Dro asked as he scanned their solemn faces. "This will take a while."

A rumble of agreement came from the eight Kings, then each man nodded.

Shaz sent a message to Elise to let her know he probably wouldn't return to office. When he laid the phone on the table, a smile stole across his lips. They'd be ready for the showdown when it came. His gaze went back to the screen and the still image of a teenager sitting on a cot with both hands wrapped around her knees, and his stomach knotted. The hopelessness in her eyes pierced him, but he pushed emotion aside. They were all committed to freeing the girls trapped inside the estate and only God in heaven could stop them. In this situation, Shaz was confident He'd be on their side. He stared at the architect's plan now captured on the screen and concentrated on Dro's words.

"After you look at these next scenes, you'll understand the bottom line is that we have to be ready to move at a moment's notice."

The slide segued into a clip of a heavily-pregnant young woman being restrained on a cot by two women, while a female nurse administered an injection. The girl stopped struggling and when she was released, tears slid down the side of her face and into her brown hair.

The nurse said something to the other two that Shaz didn't hear, then they all walked out of the narrow space. The girl—swallowed up by a hospital gown—rolled onto her side and sobbed into the pillow.

Dro was right. They couldn't wait any longer. Every minute those girls spent locked up put them at greater risk and only the Lord knew what poisons were being introduced into their system while they were incarcerated. At the same time, they had to be kept in reasonably good health if they were expected to deliver normal babies.

The Kings would have to time their entry to the Hub to take advantage of its unsuspecting clients. Even so, everything inside Shaz warned that they would be forced to execute their action plan much sooner than any of them anticipated.

CHAPTER 23

Camilla kissed Ayanna's cheek and inhaled the aroma of baby lotion and powder. The scent and cuddly warmth of her child were reassuring. No matter what was wrong in her world, the connection to Ayanna reduced everything else to insignificance.

Except for the man on the other side of the bedroom door.

Shaz had turned everything topsy-turvy in her world. She'd been careful about her emotions because of Derrick. Who wanted to have back-to-back relationships with the wrong men? She also didn't want to mistake gratitude for love, but when she was with Shaz, she forgot to guard her heart. His magnetic personality and caring attitude made taking precaution against falling for him next to impossible.

While they sat in the living room, Ayanna climbed into his lap to watch cartoons before she nodded off to sleep. When Camilla tried lifting Ayanna from Shaz's arms, she clung to him and wouldn't let go until he carried her to the bedroom and laid her in the crib. They stood watching Ayanna for a moment, then when they looked at each other the space between them disappeared. Now, as she prepared to approach him, she recalled their heated kiss and the out-of-control sensations attached to being wrapped in his arms.

Camilla didn't want him to think she was angling for another encounter. She needed to make transportation arrangements to get Ayanna to the hospital for her final visit before her procedure. A cab would do fine, but based on the security arrangements at The Castle, she doubted any outside driver would be let in without rigorous interrogation. Even then, the security team might refuse to let him inside. Plus, intuition told her Shaz would object to them getting a taxi. Since her run-in with the police, he had turned his level of protectiveness up by a thousand notches. Even during the day, Shaz ensured the security guards did intermittent checks on them. She found it disconcerting, but it made her appreciate him even more.

The carpeted alcove between her bedroom and his was bathed in shadow with only a faint light coming from the nearest window. She tapped at the door, then applied more pressure when Shaz didn't answer.

"Come in," he called.

She eased the door open and stood in the doorway as he emerged from the bathroom with a towel hanging around his waist and another around his shoulders. With one end, he dried his locs.

"You shouldn't dry your hair so vigorously," she said. "The rough treatment will break the strands."

"Too late," he said, adding a lazy grin as his gaze slid from her tank top to her lounge pants.

With both hands crossed over her chest, she leaned against the doorjamb hiding the effect of his close study on her body. "It's never too late to take good care of what God gave you."

"Agreed," he said, lowering his hand and moving steadily toward her.

The movement called attention to his abs. She wanted to touch the caramel skin covering that impressive six pack and the ridges of his chest. All too slowly, her focus returned to Shaz's face.

"I'd like to believe God gave me … you," he murmured.

Aside from an appreciative curl of the lips, his eyes glimmered and he ran one hand over his goatee. She followed its journey when it fell to his side and couldn't miss his response to her, jutting from the towel that seemed in danger of falling off his hips. She dragged her attention back to his face and pulled in a sharp breath when he threw the towel he'd been using on his hair onto a padded chair and advanced a few more feet. Camilla's first reaction was to take a step back.

His slow approach threatened to shatter what was left of her equilibrium.

"I guess you wanted to ask me something," he said, coming nearer.

Why did I come? For the life of her, Camilla couldn't get her brain to unlock the reason for this impromptu visit. She stood straight, and he stopped in front of her with mere inches separating them.

His gaze touched her everywhere before returning to settle on her lips. Shaz said nothing, but waited, as if he had all the time in the world.

An alarm beeped inside her head, and she cleared her throat. The heat from his skin reminded her how dangerously close she was standing to the sexiest man she'd ever met in her entire life. She pulled in a deep breath, inhaling the crisp citrus bath gel with a hint of jasmine and enough male pheromones to lay her flat on the floor. Then good sense returned. "I … um, I wanted to ask about transportation for tomorrow."

"What about it?" Shaz's voice emerged as a husky whisper.

"I want you …"

The easy rise and fall of his chest distracted her. Before she knew what she planned to do, she traced the line in the center and skimmed his pectoral muscles with one finger.

"You were saying?" Shaz gripped her wrist in a gentle hold, stroking her skin with his thumb.

She stepped in closer and spoke against his neck, hiding a mischievous grin. "I was saying, before you distracted me, that I wanted you to arrange—"

A gasp cut her words as Shaz drew a line up her neck with his tongue.

"Yes?" As his arms slipped around her and the length of him branded her belly, Camilla was in no doubt about where they were headed.

"A ride."

He fused his lips to her neck and sucked gently. Under his gentle ministrations, her legs threatened to give way.

"Is the hospital visit what you're trying to remember?' he whispered, lifting the fabric of her tank top to spread his hands across her back. "Or something else?"

Her laughter was soft and sultry. "You, Shaz, are a wicked man."

With soft kisses, Shaz traced a path across her jaw toward her lips. Before his mouth settled over hers, he chuckled. "I'm not aiming to prove you wrong."

He explored her mouth, stroking her tongue with his. His pace was slow and thorough, then intense, stealing her breath. As her hands came up to clasp his head, Shaz ended the kiss. Cupping her jaw, he said, "I said no pressure, and I meant it. Are you ready for this?"

"If I think about it, I'll convince myself I'm not." She inhaled, then laced her arms around his neck. "But it feels so right."

Shaz waited a few seconds before he replied, "Like I said, I'm not in the business of contradicting you." He dipped his head, and again, all rational thought dissolved as his hands roamed under her tank top.

Camilla held on to his biceps, and when he grazed the undersides of her breasts, she let out a soft moan. His long fingers stroked back and forth across the center of the soft globes, causing her knees to buckle. With one arm sealing her to his torso, Shaz moved her across the room nibbling her neck until he stood with his back to the bed.

He lifted the tank top and paused to ease it over her head. The light material fell to the floor as he sat and pressed a soft kiss to her stomach. She moaned when he flicked her navel and swirled his tongue inside.

His touch was so light, she barely felt him slipping off her pants and underwear. Then she stood naked and unashamed before him, basking in the appreciative gleam in his dark-brown eyes.

Shaz got to his feet and enclosed her in an embrace. For a moment, he did nothing other than whisper, "You're beautiful."

"And so are you."

He did a thing that she translated as rolling his eyes.

Laughing, she protested. "It's true. You are."

"Whatever you say."

He tipped her chin up and sealed his mouth to hers, going deep and forcing her to hang on to him to stay upright. Shaz gripped a handful of her behind and turned her with him so he faced the bed. "Get in, love. Lights low."

The lighting in the room dimmed as Shaz lay on his back and shifted

Camilla so she lay top of him, which brought her chest in line with his mouth. Her breath whooshed out when his lips closed around the dark-brown berry topping her breast. As he teased the bud with skillful fingers, she clasped his head, weakened by the delicious suckling motion. Before she could utter a sound, his fingers followed the line of her hip, down to her groin, and caressed the sensitive pearl at her core until she gripped handfuls of his locs and whimpered in his ear. He kept up the pressure until she convulsed and begged him to stop.

While he stretched to the bedside table, then slipped on protection, she lay with one leg thrown over his thigh. Her hands were drawn to him as if by a magnetic force and she cupped them around him, exploring new territory that was destined to be part of a delightful journey. Her teasing strokes pulled a long sigh from him.

"If you keep that up for much longer," he murmured, "What you expect to be a bang will end in a fizzle."

Despite her arousal, Camilla chuckled. "You're something else, you know that?"

Shaz nipped her ear, tickling her with his breath. "So I've been told a time or two."

She opened her mouth with the intention of telling him to shut up, but didn't get the chance. With his arm pinned across her lower back, Shaz raised his hips and entered her, searing her flesh one torturous inch at a time. Camilla closed her eyes and lowered her head, but when he was sheathed inside her, Shaz growled in his throat. "Look at me."

Camilla opened glazed eyes and focused on him.

He nodded. "Yes. Stay with me."

A slow, lazy rhythm and their intense mental connection kept Camilla tethered to Shaz, who refused to increase his pace despite Camilla digging her nails into his sides to urge him on. She was as the point of wanting to yell at him to go faster when he cupped her bottom and flipped her on her back.

Legs locked around his middle, she ground her hips into his with every powerful stroke. Perspiration dewed her skin, while sweat dripped from Shaz's forehead onto her chest.

Each time her inner muscles massaged him, Shaz thrust harder and his breath tickled her ear. The brush of his locs against her sensitive skin added to the sensory overload engulfing her. As their skin clung and released, a tiny flame started at her core and spread outward, threatening to explode and send her careening as far away as the island she'd come from.

Shaz let out a roar and continued plunging into her as she arched against him and let herself go. Her legs trembled uncontrollably as shockwaves spread outward from her center and flung her into space.

A starburst of color showered behind her eyelids as Shaz's heart thundered against hers. His harsh inhalation and slow, prolonged thrusts sent her crashing headlong into another orgasm. With his name as a keening cry on her lips, Camilla descended from an incredible high.

Shaz shifted them until she lay with her head on his chest. Minutes passed with her listening to the slowing pace of his breathing. He pushed the hair off her forehead and gathered her to his chest. Their lips met in a soft, sweet kiss that evolved into what Camilla could only describe as a meeting of souls at a level she'd never experienced with anyone else.

The soothing caresses to her hair made her want to wrap herself around Shaz and cuddle for the rest of the night, but the insistent pressure from his erection prodding her inner thigh told her they were headed in the opposite direction.

CHAPTER 24

The muted buzz of the phone woke Shaz. He untangled his legs and removed his arm from Camilla's grip. In the darkness, he kissed the smooth skin of her cheek.

Her last-minute transportation request had created the leeway for the consummation of their relationship. The sight of her in lounge pants and tank top had reignited the fire below his waist that he'd been beating back for a week since she moved into his suite. After a night of mind-blowing sex, he refused to let her leave his bed.

He rolled over and reached for the cellular on the bedside table.

Reno's voice was crisp and clear, as if it was nine o' clock in the morning instead of an ungodly hour of the night. "It certainly took you long enough. You need to get down to the boardroom."

Searching his mind, he asked, "Did I miss a notice for a meeting?"

"Just get down here and wear something dark."

"Who're you talking to?" Camilla mumbled, while settling her hips against his crotch.

"Castle business." Shaz dropped another kiss on her jaw and ignored the fullness at his groin. He rolled off the bed, yanked out the bureau drawer, then stepped into his underwear, his mind taken up with what could have happened while he slept. "I have to go."

Camilla sat up and switched on the bedside lamp. "In the dead of night?"

His gaze shot to the alarm clock. "Actually, it's 3:00 a.m."

"Same thing." Camilla flopped down on the sheets watching him.

"Don't worry." He pulled on a navy sweater and a pair of black jeans, then dropped the medallion in his pocket. "We'll talk when I get back."

Yawning, she swung her feet over the side of the mattress. As she pulled on her panties and tank top, Camilla mumbled, "I'm going to check on Ayanna and get back in my own bed. See you when you return."

In a few strides, he made it to where she stood with her pants hanging over one shoulder. He wrapped both arms around her and spoke against her mouth. "Check on Ayanna, but when I return if you're not here, I'm coming to find you."

She slid her arms up his chest and circled his neck, tugging one of his locs. With a sultry whisper, she asked, "Is that a promise?"

"You betcha." He kissed her neck, then her mouth and her forehead. "Later."

Her sinuous walk held his attention until his phone beeped another time. He'd received a text message from Reno.

If you don't get here in five, we convene without you. Come armed.

Inside the closet, Shaz accessed the safe, extracted a Glock 43 and strapped it to his leg. With a leather band taming his hair and ankle boots on his feet, Shaz left the wing containing his suite and sprinted to the main building, then made the trip downstairs. He stepped inside the boardroom with ten seconds to spare.

Seven Kings stood around the table, dressed the same as Shaz— dark, long-sleeved sweaters and pants, plus heavy shoes.

Kaleb walked into the room a second behind Shaz and they all took their seats.

"Now that everybody's here, let's go." Vikkas turned to the wall behind him and the doors silently slid open. One click to the remote brought the screen to life. "I know we were here earlier to agree on strategic moves regarding New Visions and The Hub, but Daron alerted me to suspicious movement there a short while ago. We have to accelerate our timeline."

"This feels like we've dropped in the middle of a spy drama," Kaleb said, frowning.

"Call it what you will, but what is certain is that we have to get moving." Vikkas turned his gaze on Shaz. "You've been digging up graves and they've been trying to move the bodies. They took some of the girls out of the facility just after midnight."

Vikkas held up one hand when they shifted in a wave, as if to rise. "Don't lose it, they're in safekeeping. That threat was neutralized by Daron and his team. It's time to do a clean sweep of the property before the rest of them realize what's happened."

The atmosphere was charged. Shaz put the adrenaline flowing through his system into words. "I take it we're moving right now."

Reno rose from the table and glanced at his watch. "That's a yes. Once we're inside The Hub, we'll notify Jason Stone of what we find. He'll bring in a law enforcement team and they will shut down everything inside those buildings."

"Jason Stone?" Dwayne frowned. "Why does that name sound familiar?"

"Cameron's brother," Daron said, referencing his woman.

"If this is urgent, what are we waiting for?" Dro asked.

"That's what I want to know, too," Kaleb said, to a rumble of agreement from the other Kings.

"Fact is, there are certain *players,* for want of a better term." Reno grimaced, then continued, "that we will catch red-handed. Then there are others that, even now, are on their way into The Hub. Those are big wigs in this city as well. We can ruin this by being too gung-ho, or we can wait until those other men get here. If we're patient and shut them down, we'll be rid of at least four tentacles on this Hydra."

Kaleb grimaced at the reference to the multiple-headed serpent from Greek mythology with the ability to regenerate its head once it was severed. Nodding slowly, he announced, "I'm with you. The sensible course would be to wait."

Reno dipped his head in approval. "In a couple of minutes, we'll head across and do what we have to do. We'll enter the building based on our earlier plans." Scanning each of them, he stated, "I trust you came equipped, as instructed."

When they nodded, he continued, "Shaz, you'll want to be in position out front at The Hub when the FBI rolls in, since one of the main shareholders, plus his sidekick, is in residence and they're about to be *entertained* as we speak. I'm sure you won't mind seeing the back of them."

As Vikkas powered down the screen, Daron added, "We didn't want to turn your stomach, so we opted not to show you that footage."

With a finger to his earpiece, Daron pointed to the credenza where an electronic bank of radios stood. "Grab one each. The channel is already set. Test them and let's go. Be careful and remember not to pull your weapon unless you intend to use it."

They did as instructed, then used two elevators to access the ground floor and avoided the foyer despite the hour of the morning. Anything that concerned The Castle drew media attention and when things happened, the newshounds appeared as if summoned by magic.

The Kings converged on the headquarters of The Hub, accessing the building through designated entrances and exits, using stealth and aided by Daron's gadgets.

Dro, Dwayne, and Shaz crept into an elegant marble lobby, furnished with plush sofas and heavy glass tables. The smile on the pretty blonde faded when they eased up to the counter. She shot out of her seat, frowning at them. "Can I help you gentlemen?"

"Don't touch anything," Dro said, as she reached for something below their eye level. "Otherwise you'll be in more trouble than you're already in."

Her gaze darted between them, but she laid both hands on the marble surface as her face flushed.

Shaz's lips quirked into a humourless smile. "Good decision."

Daron, Grant, and Kaleb swept past them, along with several other men clad in black vests with FBI lettering.

As they disappeared down the nearest corridor, Dro turned his attention back to the receptionist, dropping the black knapsack he carried on the counter. "You're going to let us into your space, but don't do anything foolish."

She nodded quickly and used one hand to hit a button.

A series of low beeps sounded as they let themselves into the area behind the reception desk.

At the same time, a door opened behind the blonde. She threw a panicked look over her shoulder, then back at Dro as a pair of security guards stepped forward and flanked her. The two males were cookie-cutter images—tall, brawny, bald-headed with ruddy complexions. On spotting the three Kings, both men pulled their weapons.

Shaz reflexively drew the Glock and leveled it at one of the guards. Dwayne did the same with the other. Time hadn't allowed for any target practice recently but Shaz figured if his aim was off at this distance, he deserved to have his firearm license revoked.

"Think very carefully about your next move, unless you have a death wish." Dro shifted to one side, his 9mm Sig Sauer handgun drawn. His pitch remained cool and unhurried for someone who'd just been in the flight path of four bullets. "In which case, my colleagues will be quite happy to oblige. They're crack shots."

"Not to mention the fact that you're outnumbered," Shaz added. "The bigger question is this. Are you willing to die for the scuzzballs who employ you?"

The tense seconds stretched and none of the men stood down.

The receptionist hyperventilated with her back pressed to the wall.

"Let me put it to you this way," Dwayne said, from his position next to Shaz. "This standoff can be easily resolved. You lower your weapons and we bring this to a close without anyone getting hurt. I'm a peaceful man … my brothers here, not so much."

When the guards didn't give an inch, Dwayne continued. "You know what? I'm always willing to try something different. My first bullet is about to land in someone's ass. Let's see which of you will cop that honor."

After a silent exchange that lasted a few seconds, both guards let their hands fall to their sides.

With his gun, Shaz motioned to them. "Put your weapons on that table and take a seat."

Dro reached into his knapsack then approached both men, who sat in disapproving silence while he confined their hands with plastic handcuffs. That done, Dro, Dwayne, and Shaz scanned the electronic display board on which several lighted buttons blinked at intervals.

Shaz crooked a finger at the receptionist, who tottered toward him from her position against the wall. Pointing to the unit, he said, "This tells which rooms are occupied?"

The tall woman nodded.

If the lights told a truthful tale, at least a dozen clients were in-house.

"What's over here?" He pointed to an elongated block that pulsed with eight circular crimson lights.

She stiffened. "I'm not allowed to say."

Shaz exchanged a glance with Dro, who was using the radio. As his mind flashed back to their earlier meeting, he had a brain wave. Daron had mentioned a black-out area he hadn't been able to crack and see inside to determine what activity happened there. Shaz had his suspicions. Settling his weight on both feet, he folded his arms. "What's your name?"

"It's Angie," she said, flipping hair over her shoulder.

"Think about this, Angie." Shaz enunciated his words so she wouldn't miss anything he said. "Things will go much easier if you cooperate. I'll remember that you helped us when this cesspool goes public and your role in it is exposed."

She gasped, "But I'm only an employee."

He tipped one brow. "Who's aware of what's happening in her place of employment and is complicit with her bosses' illegal activities."

"But—"

"Spare me." He raised both hands. "We need access to this place. Where is it?"

Angie rubbed her forehead, then lowered her head. "It's behind a wall that's located beyond where we—they keep the pregnant girls."

"D'you have the code for those rooms?"

She shook her head. "No, the security personnel do."

"Thank you." He unclipped the radio from his belt and with his eyes on Dro and Dwayne, conveyed what he learned to Daron.

The staccato beat of footsteps came from the corridor, along with the Alderman's protests. The disheveled politician was secured between two FBI agents, who frogmarched him toward the entrance.

Shaz's only pang of sympathy was for the Alderman's family, who would not be spared in the backlash from his activities within The Castle walls.

Angie gasped, then covered her mouth with both hands.

"What are you staring at?" Bennett bellowed. "Get Milholland on the phone. Now!"

Turning to one of the agents restraining him, he barked, "This is outrageous. I demand to speak with my lawyer. All of this is unnecessary." His gaze fell on Shaz and a ripple went through his body. He came to a stop despite the officers flanking him. "This is your fault. *You* did this. You're going to be sorry."

"Not as sorry as you'll be where you're going," Shaz warned, then gave him a mock salute.

From behind them another wave of disturbance arose, and Shaz drawled, "Here comes your lawyer now. Good luck with negotiating your case. Since the two of you might be cell buddies, you'll have the chance to compare notes."

Milholland was as rumpled as his client, with wisps of hair sticking out from the fringe around his head. His pale eyes darted to his client, who was still throwing threats.

"This isn't finished," Bennett snarled. "You'll hear from me."

"You and your threats." Shaz looked him up and down and let contempt drip from his voice. "Use them on someone who give a rat's ass about them."

By the time the two men left the building, almost dragged by the agents, Shaz was thinking he might not need to put Georgiana through the trauma of testifying since Milholland had also been caught with one of the girls.

As FBI agents perp-walked more than a dozen influential businessmen and politicians out of the gentleman's club, Shaz wondered about the compulsion that led them to put their freedom and reputation at risk when they all had families.

The last person to be led out was Angie, who was weeping by that time.

Shaz rubbed his eyes that were grainy from the lack of sleep and the indulgences with Camilla last night. He was bone tired, but had one other matter to deal before he could rest.

The other individuals inside who were still imprisoned, as well as the missing girl. Nicole.

CHAPTER 25

On his way to The Harem—as the holding area for the girls had been labeled—Shaz identified himself to FBI agents and police officers. None of the Kings were allowed inside while another team of FBI agents—including several females—processed that part of the building.

Ten minutes later, after he, Reno, and Dwayne had a mini-conference in the back lounge of The Hub, Shaz moved into position as an agent led the girls out and made them sit in what had formerly served as a waiting and transit area before they were sent to their assigned client. While he waited, Shaz pulled up Nicole's image on his phone.

The girl he was looking for was short, with bright eyes and a dark complexion. He hung back, leaning against the maroon accent wall. She was the last to emerge, looking gloomy and shaken with her arms wrapped around her body.

He stepped forward and kept his hands in his pockets. These girls had been abused, and he didn't want to inflict even one additional moment of stress. He kept his voice pitched low. "Nicole?"

She tipped her head back and moved sideways out of his reach. "Yes?"

"Georgiana gave me your name."

Still skittish, she stood away from him. With her brows furrowed, she asked, "Who?"

He pointed toward where she'd been kept. "She was in here and escaped weeks ago."

"Oh." After a moment, a tiny smile shone through. "She kept her promise. She said she'd tell somebody I was here."

"Yeah." Shaz smiled back at her. "Your mother asked me to look for you."

Nicole shrank back and reverted to Patois. "She know me in here?"

"Yes, she knows you're here."

"She goin' to kill me." Tears streamed down her face and she looked up at him.

Shaz didn't think it was wise to touch her although she clearly needed to be comforted. Instead, he stooped and looked up at her. "Listen to me. The only thing on your mother's mind is having you back. Stop worrying. I'm going to call her, so she can be on spot when you're released, okay?"

Nicole grimaced as if she didn't believe things would work out that easily, then whispered, "Thanks."

As a female agent pointed her toward the waiting area, Shaz closed his eyes. His mother had told him never to turn his back on a good opportunity. He'd done exactly that the first time Khalil reached out to him and look how that turned out. Thankfully, he was now in a position to right those wrongs alongside his brothers.

His blood brother crossed his mind, but Shaz set Martin's problems aside to figure out later. His heart contracted as another set of girls, each of them in various stages of pregnancy, filed through the passage toward him. This scenario was exactly what he expected to find after Georgiana's revelation, plus the details he uncovered. None of the girls looked older than sixteen. All of them seemed lost. Blank stares and hopeless eyes greeted him from their faces.

Dwayne, Dro, Grant, Reno, and Shaz exchanged pained stares. Through his expertise in the solutions side of domestic abuse and providing shelter for disadvantaged women, Reno would be able to help with housing.

When the last of them left with the agent, Shaz faced the doorway leading to the cells. "There's one more thing we have to do before they take the guards away."

"What's that?" Dro asked as they all fell in step with him.

"You'll see."

He strode to an office behind the back wall, where agents were in the process of combing the room, which housed several desks, chairs, and a similar control panel to the one behind the reception counter. A quick study confirmed this edition was more sophisticated.

After introducing himself and his brothers to the man in charge, Shaz stated his case. "Somewhere along this wall is an entrance to another part of this set up. My guess is based on what I saw on the electronic system at reception."

With his thick eyebrows pulled together, the brawny redhead folded his arms and glowered at the four beefy female guards standing along one wall. "What will we find?" he asked.

Shaz angled his chin toward the seemingly flat surface behind the man. "Agent McClausky, I suspect there are little ones back there."

His eyebrows shot toward his hairline and he took in the other FBI agents, who now stood motionless, in one sweep. "You mean like a nursery?"

"Exactly."

Abruptly, Agent McClausky moved toward the guards, pacing in front of them. When he spoke, his voice thundered. "You. Step forward."

The tall, heavyset woman was expressionless.

Agent McClausky pointed to the table with the computer equipment. "Open the paneling."

She didn't move immediately, and a humorless smile twisted Agent McClausky's lips. "You better think about making things easy on yourself, since as of right now, you're in a hard place."

Her lips twisted in a smirk. "In case you missed it, I'm only an employee here."

McClausky shook his head. "You better get in line with that sad excuse. This must be the fifth time I've heard that tonight. You'd be singing a different song if one of these girls was your daughter."

His words seemed to deflate her and she turned away and faced the desk. In a series of key taps, she put in a command.

Before their eyes, the entire wall retracted and a set of double doors with frosted glass appeared. Nobody moved until Agent McClausky barked, "Open it,"

Two agents surged through the doors ahead of him, and the Kings followed.

A pair of wide-eyed nurses, wearing hairnets and surgical masks spun away from them.

"Federal Agents. Do. Not. Move."

Trembling, the women stared at the men surrounding them as they were made to sit in a far corner, furnished with a central table and visitor's chairs.

The brightly-lit room contained a row of cribs along one wall and on the other, a set of incubators. Digital display panels lit the equipment connected to each incubator.

Shaz hovered over each less than a second and was shocked to find six of them occupied by infants of various ethnicities. Only two cribs contained babies. "Where are the mothers?" he asked one of the nurses.

"Let us ask the questions, Mr. Bostwick," Agent McClausky said. "Most likely they have them at another location. We'll treat their welfare as a matter of urgency."

He cracked a smile. "Now that you've dropped more work in our laps, you and these gentlemen should give us a chance to request more personnel to process this area. We need to let Agent Stone know of these developments."

"No need for that," Jason said, walking into the room. "I heard."

He shook hands with each of the Kings and after a brief conversation, promised to update them as much as he was able to, under the circumstances.

By the end of the round-up and processing of various individuals, it was 7:00 a.m.

The Kings all stood in the foyer of the main building of The Castle. Similarly dressed, and in various stages of exhaustion, they looked like a battalion of war-weary soldiers. In a sense, they were. Hand in his pocket, Shaz fingered the medallion with a sense of satisfaction. This was the reason he did what he did. To right wrongs and be of service to his fellowmen.

With a half-smile on his face, Shaz went through and did a man hug with each, clapping them on the back and expressing his thanks for the night just past and again for their overall support. They weren't family by blood, but they made a heck of a lot of difference in helping him shut down a small slice of the evil that had invaded the Castle. Dro and Daron were now tasked with following leads to see how far that trail went.

Shaz had a couple of things to conclude to make Bennett's case air-tight, then he'd be free and clear to put the finishing touches on his personal agenda.

CHAPTER 26

Before he held the car door open, Shaz brushed Camilla's lips with his. Then he went in deep, as if he hadn't kissed her two minutes ago.

They stood outside the Chicago O'Hare International Airport, where people waited curbside for pickup and some breezed past them, getting in and out of cabs.

Ayanna pulled his shirt sleeve, and he looked into her bright eyes. She held her arms open and wriggled her fingers. "Sha, kiss!"

Laughing, he took her from Camilla's side and smacked her cheek. "Happy now?"

She grabbed his jaw and started a conversation. In the past few weeks, he'd gotten more fluent in her baby talk, but still had a way to go.

Camilla tried removing her from his arms, but she protested.

"It's okay," he said, rubbing Ayanna's back. "I'll strap her in."

While he did, Camilla watched him. She kissed his cheek when he stood straight. "Thanks. Soon, she won't want me to do anything for her."

"She's a sweetie," he said as Camilla sat in the passenger seat. He threw Ayanna a kiss over his shoulder. "And she knows what she wants. Right, Ayanna?"

She giggled and squeezed the rag doll she carried close to her chest.

Behind the wheel, he looked across at Camilla. "Let's go home and then over to Mom's."

"Do we have enough time?" she asked, glancing at her watch.

"Yeah, they won't be ready to eat for another couple of hours."

"As long as you tell Miss Paula this was your plan," Camilla said, giving him a doubtful look.

He patted her thigh and met her gaze for a second. "You worry too much."

"With good reason sometimes."

Shooting her another glance, he said. "There's never a good reason to worry. As long as you're taking steps to resolve your problems, worrying is a waste of time. Thursday was a case in point."

She shrugged and looked over her shoulder at Ayanna. "I'll give you that."

"Baby girl, you know I'm right."

Camilla stroked his locs and rubbed his jaw with the back of her hand. "Okay, so you were right this time. Don't be getting a big head over it."

"Says you." He waited a moment before licking his lip and putting the icing on his statement. "When you're good, you're good."

Two days ago, they went to the U.S. Embassy in Kingston, Jamaica, and had Camilla's visa successfully renewed. Dro and Vikkas had laid the groundwork for her eventual application for a green card, which would allow her to work in the States. Shaz had already started wrapping his mind about having Camilla with him on a permanent basis.

Among the other things they did was to visit Camilla's mother, who thanked Shaz for taking care of her two girls. Ayanna's pediatrician conducted a thorough physical. After looking at several x-ray images, she offered good wishes for the upcoming procedure for the baby. At their request, she supplied a dossier with Ayanna's medical history addressed to Jai.

With business completed, they spent just over twenty-four hours in Montego Bay, where Camilla met Shaz's grandmother and the extended family. He even managed to get in a couple rounds of golf at the Sandals and Half Moon courses in Ocho Rios and Montego Bay.

He waited for Camilla's response, thinking she was a trooper.

She rolled her eyes, laughed, and looked out the window. A moment later, she said, "Despite your big head, I'm still gonna say thanks. You've done so much to make things fall into place."

"That's what significant others do, sweets." He tapped her chin, then put his hand back on the wheel. "And still there's more to complete, but don't worry about it. The most important thing is that Bennett is out of your life."

"Yes. Thank God for that. At times, I wondered if we'd win the fight." She pulled in a deep breath, then rested a hand on his leg. "I don't think I'd have made it had he succeeded in adopting my daughter."

"We agreed you wouldn't keep bothering your brain about that. We'll let everything take its course and deal with Porter's paternity rights at the opportune time. I don't have to tell you how honored I'd be if you let me give Ayanna my name."

Her breath caught, then with a beautiful smile accompanying her words, she whispered, "I think we'd both be honored, too."

They fell into a comfortable silence that was broken only when Shaz eased into his designated parking spot. Touching her cheek, he said, "This is the part where we drop our things and head across town."

Ayanna had fallen asleep, so while Shaz brought their things inside, Camilla freshened her up and did the same for herself. When she emerged from the bathroom, Shaz took her place. As he dried his face, his gaze fell on a bright yellow duckling on the face basin and the tiny pink toothbrush in the cup. He couldn't help chuckling. Ayanna was the smallest person in the suite, but her things were everywhere. He'd never lived in close proximity to a child before, but he kinda liked it and hoped there were a few more in his future.

"You better get moving." Camilla walked in and hugged him around the waist. "I don't want your mama mad at me for keeping her apart from her favorite son."

Shaz grinned at Camilla in the mirror. "Mom tells all of us we're her favorite son."

As her eyes danced, Camilla sassed him. "That's beside the point."

He turned to pull her into his embrace. Dropping kisses on her cheek, he mumbled, "You have her eating out of your hand, so I can get away with anything."

Shaz buried his face in the side of her neck and as his desire for her rose, he backed her against the wall. They exchanged a searing kiss that left Camilla's eyes glazed, and him even more aroused. His voice was hoarse as he said, "What about if we—"

Before he finished his proposal, Camilla shook her head slowly. "No. Nope. Nada. That has to be later." She wriggled sideways out of his embrace. "Later will be greater, as they say."

He slapped her butt as he followed her into the bedroom. "You're mean, not to mention corny."

"Whatever," she threw over her shoulder. "I want to be alive to see my daughter grow up."

He caught Camilla's hand and turned her into his body. With one arm, he anchored her to him. "Me too. Plus, the other kids we're gonna have if you're up to giving me a whole tribe of Bostwicks."

Camilla's wide eyes gave away her shock. "Um. You don't do anything by half measures, do you?"

"No, ma'am." He rested his forehead against hers. "Not when it comes to you."

Whatever she intended to say was cut off when Ayanna wandered into the room rubbing her eyes. "Mommy?"

"I thought you put her in the crib," he said.

"Again, you should have consulted me before running out and buying that crib by yourself." Camilla laughed as she lifted Ayanna. "I did put her inside, but she's an escape artist. She climbed over the railing."

An hour and a half later, they were seated in the Bostwick's yard drinking fish tea—a thin soup with fish as the base, served as an appetizer. They followed that up with curried goat.

The kids ran around the yard, refusing to eat in their excitement, but Paula made it known they wouldn't escape for long.

Her contented smile as she watched her grandchildren made it obvious to Shaz that his mother was happy. His father had a low-key mellow vibe going on, too, whistling as he doled out a cup of soup to Roman, who showed up after everyone else. Shaz wondered what news their parents planned to lay on them today.

His gaze shifted to Martin, who was more relaxed than Shaz had seen him in a long time. Come to think of it, even Sondra looked like she had a secret. His gaze went to her loaded plate and he covered his mouth to hide a grin. Shaz reached for Camilla's hand. In a while, they'd have news of their own too. Just as his parents knew they were meant for each other early in their relationship, he was convinced Camilla would be his wife.

When Roman grabbed a lawn chair and sat across from Shaz, he eyed him with suspicion. "If you weren't scowling as you usually do when you're thinking, I'd think I was in the wrong yard. Why's everybody so happy?"

Even Martin laughed in response to his question.

"Good question, son." Teddy wiped his hands on a dish towel and sat between them. "We're proud and still happy about the massive takedown that Shaz and his brothers organized at The Castle. Your mother and I didn't quite realize the depth of what he was doing over there."

His explanation relieved Shaz. Despite his advice to Camilla not to worry about what she couldn't change, he'd been uneasy about the outcome of this visit. With any luck, his parents would now be prepared to forget about him being active in the business.

"It's crazy, the stuff that's in the news," Martin added with a scowl. "It's an epidemic that's been spreading for years. Remember the hundreds of people arrested in Canada in that international child pornography ring? There were foster parents, doctors, nurses, teachers, and law enforcement personnel involved."

"And as if that wasn't enough," their father chimed in, "There was that bust in Florida recently. Over a hundred people arrested for human trafficking."

"Disgraceful," Paula said, as she walked up to them. "Those poor girls and women. You don't know who to trust."

"That's true," Shaz said, "Imagine being let down by those society deem trustworthy."

"Thank God they were rescued."

Roman gave Shaz a thumbs up. "I have to admit, you've done good, little brother, and I know you put your all into taking care of your clients. Sorry about … well, you know what."

"All is forgiven," Shaz said. "I know you're a knucklehead."

Shaz ignored Roman's glare and concentrated on his father's words.

"That's enough, you two." With a proud smile in place, Teddy nodded toward his eldest child. "Martin and I have been working through a familiarization process at the firm and he's giving up his job at the end of the month."

Shaz wanted to do a fist pump, but that would have been extra. Instead, he let a wide grin speak for him.

Paula stood next to Teddy, rubbing his shoulder. "That puts us closer to going on that trip and leaving you young'uns in charge."

Shaz and Roman exchanged a glance, then turned their gazes on Martin, who flushed and gave them a sheepish grin. Then he said, "After our talk at the last barbeque, I did some personal restructuring to accommodate our family business."

"We also have some news." He laced his fingers with Sondra's and looked sideways at her. "We're gonna have a baby."

"That would account for all that food you're eating," Roman said, then yelped when Venetia dug her elbow into his side and hissed in his ear. Frowning, he sipped from his cup. "What? If you can't be honest with family …"

When the congratulations and noise settled, Shaz made an announcement. "Speaking of food, Grandma sent back a sweet potato pudding with us."

Paula put a hand to her hip. "Why are you holding it prisoner?"

While Camilla stifled laughter, Shaz protested. "It's on top of the fridge."

"No doubt because you intended to eat half of it, after we stuffed ourselves full of coconut cake." Paula's words were accompanied by a mock glare.

"I may be sly," Shaz quipped, "but I'm not desperate. Grandma gave me one of my own. That one is safe at my place."

As the children shouted a nursery rhyme, interrupting their conversation, Shaz chuckled. These were the changes to come in his future. A full, noisy household. A family that thrived on togetherness. The complexities of The Castle. And a woman at his side to help him balance all of that.

Yes, the future looked incredible.

CHAPTER 27

"Your talk was sharp, to the point, and hit home with those boys," Shaz said, tipping a glass of club soda toward Dwayne.

He responded by clinking his glass of water against Shaz's. "If you're saying thank you, then you're welcome."

They shared a chuckle as the other Kings filtered into the board room for their weekly meeting. When all nine of them were seated, Vikkas called the meeting to order.

Each man provided an update on the main business at hand. Despite all the ground they covered each week, the assassination attempt remained the first order of business. Everything else came after they studied the evidence uncovered and used their impressive range of skills to analyze the data and draw conclusions.

"Shaz, you want to tell us where you are on your findings to do with New Visions and The Elite Hub?"

He pulled up a file on his iPad and scrolled down the screen. "Since my last report, we've confirmed that Bennett was the mastermind behind the illegal activity taking place in both organizations. For New Visions, there were a few adoptions that were on the level. All the contracts in good order. Duly signed and notarized as required by law."

Before continuing his report, he scanned the face of each King. "And there were others."

Shaz went on to outline a scheme wherein Bennett took advantage of troubled young women he came in contact with through the various outreach programs around Evanston. Once he reeled in the girls, a select few catered to the needs of The Hub's clients. Others who were pregnant and had nowhere to go, were kept inside the property and their babies bought by those who could pay a premium price for newborns—despite what the girls wanted. Sick to his stomach, he confirmed the baby found in the dumpster was also part of an organ harvesting outfit designed to use and abuse the unfortunate.

When the rumble of anger and disgust settled, the room went silent.

"So, if he was picking up girls in desperate situations," Kaleb said, tapping his stylus against the table, "he had a never-ending cash cow."

"Something like that," Shaz agreed. "The worst part is that with the other girls, depending on the needs of his clients, he was getting them from off-shore, too. There were girls from different nationalities, and it was only by contact with one client that I found out about that Jamaican girl.

"And I should tell you, the mothers of those babies we found are getting a second chance with going back to school and all that." He paused, then added, "One wasn't so lucky. She didn't survive childbirth, but I'm sure the feds will make Bennett pay for that, especially since she was underage, and there's a rumor that he was the father of her baby."

"Bad business," Dro said, shaking his head. "The only consolation is that he's going to pay big time, along with his cohorts."

Daron looked up from his phone. "Remember that guy who picked up Camilla?"

Shaz dipped his head once, and Daron continued, "He's the Alderman's nephew, who was running around doing his dirty work."

"Dang." Shaz snapped his fingers. "The two of them do have a resemblance. For the life of me I knew he seemed familiar, but I couldn't place him. With the information you got out of him, Bennett and Milholland are taking a one-way trip to federal prison."

"That's two tentacles chopped off," Vikkas said, looking up from his iPad. "Who knows how many more there are in total. Good job, guys. You're all in one piece and no shots fired. I'd say we're doing mighty good. If there's nothing else, can someone move for the termination—"

Three hands went up and several men said, "I," in concert.

As they streamed out of the conference room, Dro asked Shaz. "What about Porter? How does he figure in all this?"

"Trust, the police dragnet didn't miss him. Turns out, he was involved in trafficking girls from Jamaica. That girl, Nicole. She was one of his victims."

"How's Camilla dealing with it?" Dro faced him when they stopped at the end of the corridor.

"The only thing that bothers her is that he's connected to her daughter in any way. Since he was so eager to give up his paternity rights for the adoption to move forward, she's biding her time about getting him to relinquish any claims to Ayanna."

"What about the adoption?" Dro asked, frowning.

"That's the weirdest thing. I've searched high and low in the document centre and the data bank and there's no trace of that paperwork." Shaz raised both brows then smirked. "And a little birdie told me the records stashed at Milholland's office can't be found either. It's almost as if the file was spirited out of the building. Disappeared into the four winds."

"I won't even ask how that's possible," Dro said, returning his smirk.

They stepped into the sunshine and Shaz turned his face up to the afternoon sun. "It's better if you don't. Ya know, just in case some ish hits the fan."

His phone rang and he eased it out to look at the screen. "Anyway, I gotta go, Ayanna's procedure is this afternoon. Wish us luck."

"You got it." As he walked away, he added, "Tell Camilla I'm rooting for all of you."

Giving him a thumbs up sign, Shaz answered the call, "Hey, babe. You ready to roll?"

She sounded breathless. "Yes, as ready as we'll ever be."

"You okay, babe?"

"I think so." After a beat of time, she said, "I'll be even better when you get here."

Hands in his pockets, Shaz hurried toward his suite. Five minutes later, he stood in the open doorway with Ayanna in his arms. Camilla emerged from the bedroom with a small suitcase. "Just in case we have to overnight for some reason," she said, tipping to kiss his cheek.

Camilla said nothing on the ride to the hospital, except for when Miss Mabel called to ask how they were getting on. As they went into the facility with Ayanna in Shaz's arms, Camilla dragged her feet like someone going to the gallows.

Taking her hand in his, Shaz kissed her knuckles. "Honey, it's gonna be okay. The doctors explained everything to your satisfaction, correct?"

"Yes, but—"

"No buts, like Mom would say, have a little faith. God will do the rest."

Camilla stayed strong up to the point where Ayanna was anesthetised. When the attendant wheeled the stretcher away, Camilla turned aside, blotting her eyes with the heels of her hand.

Sighing at his inability to bring comfort, Shaz gave her his handkerchief. "Come on, hon. Let's go back to the waiting room."

They went down a short corridor and when Shaz pushed the door open, Camilla gasped.

Aside from her cousin, Stacey, Denise, Paula and Teddy sat around the small space. Even Miss Mabel made an appearance, but seemed about to weep at Camilla's state.

Paula got to her feet and hugged Camilla. "Don't cry. This is what family is for. It'll be okay."

Camilla nodded and sat next to Paula, who kept an arm around her. Miss Mabel bolstered her from the other end of the seat.

Deep inside, Shaz was disturbed over the picture the doctor had painted for them. The hospital had reconsidered their approach and opted to do a cardiac catheterization, which was less invasive. Shaz didn't see how inserting a tube from the baby's groin sounded any less drastic, but at least they wouldn't be opening Ayanna's chest. Without him realizing it, the toddler had also grown on him and he couldn't imagine life without her. As he paced, he sent up a prayer that everything would go smoothly. They hadn't come this far to even think about any kind of roadblock.

A short time later, disruption came in the form of the other Kings flowing into the waiting area like a living tide of testosterone. Stacey and Denise's eyes widened as they observed the group of powerful males, who each paid their respect to the Bostwicks, then Miss Mabel, and finally, Shaz and Camilla. Some of the Kings sat and others leaned against the walls in quiet conversation as they waited with the family.

In between comforting Camilla, Shaz stayed on his feet. When he'd walked the corridors for the hundredth time—all while receiving encouragement from his fellow Kings—a middle-aged doctor in scrubs approached the group. With a cheerful smile, he announced, "Miss Gibson, the procedure was successful. Ayanna came through it with no complications. You can see her in twenty minutes. She's now in the recovery area. She'll be sleepy for a while, but she'll be fine."

"Thank, God," Camilla whispered as she hugged Paula.

Shaz wrapped his arms around Camilla as she wept. Stroking her back, he whispered. "Come on now, hon, we got good news."

"I know," she said, sniffing into his chest. "The stress of everything kinda wore me down."

"I understand." He stared into her eyes, still holding her close. "But trust me, honey, you haven't seen anything yet. All our good days are ahead of us."

She dredged up a watery smile. "I guess so."

"Have I failed you, or Ayanna, yet?"

Camilla's smile was brighter. "No, I can't say you have."

"Watch me. From here on in, things will only get better."

CHAPTER 28

Ayanna's age influenced the doctors' decision to keep her overnight.

Shaz and Camilla remained at the hospital and convinced the other members of the family that it was fine for them to go home. For the rest of the evening, Shaz and Camilla took turns sitting at the bedside and napping in the chairs provided. Shaz insisted on Ayanna being placed in a private room, so the three of them would be comfortable.

At dawn, he roused Camilla by touching his lips to hers. "I'm going home to get ready for work. Call me when she wakes," he ordered.

Camilla let her arms slip from around his neck after she kissed him a second time. "I will."

Although he had back-to-back meetings for much of the day, he called several times for updates. At the end of the day, when the doctors agreed Ayanna could go home, Shaz met them at the hospital.

The family had returned to visit, so Shaz ordered dinner and everybody drove back to The Castle in a convoy.

Shaz arrived first, got out of the vehicle, and picked up Ayanna, who immediately rested her head against his shoulder. She was drowsy from pain medication given for discomfort at the catheter insertion site, but clutched one of his locs in her fist.

Turning a worried gaze on the toddler and laying the back of her hand against her skin, Camilla said, "I think you should get her inside. I'll wait for the others to catch up."

Shaz couldn't help teasing her. "Are you sure the doctors explained the recovery process to you? You still look worried."

"Just testing if she has a fever." She tugged one of his locs. "I'm trying, okay?"

"Ow! That hurts, woman."

Camilla cut him with a bad look. "Stop messing with me then."

Laughing, Shaz shook his head. "I know who can't stand *mouthing*, as Jamaicans call it."

"Gimmie my baby." Camilla stood next to him, clearly trying not to laugh. She took the little girl, but Ayanna waved her hands toward him. "Want Sha."

He preened, dusted his jacket, then reached for Ayanna and kissed her cheek. "See, my baby knows who's the man." He kissed Ayanna's forehead and, after a moment, handed her back. "Wait for me," he said, as the other cars rolled in behind them.

The family members parked their vehicles, then Shaz led the way to the suite and welcomed them inside.

Camilla's cousin oohed and aahed over the suite, while his family made a beeline for the kitchen. Shaz leaned in the doorway watching his mother supervise the housekeeping staff, even as she uncovered various food containers.

"Oh. My. Lord."

Camilla's exclamation startled Shaz and he headed for Ayanna's room with the family on his heels. When they stood in the doorway, several gasps came from behind him.

The room was filled with balloons in the colors of the rainbow. A kaleidoscope of cartoon characters covered the bed. Ayanna sat in the centre, laughing as she examined her new toys. The crib on the other side of the bedroom was crammed with character balloons. Nine of them, in a cluster of metallic shades, including his favorite navy blue, were anchored to a huge basket filled with a range of fruits. Each balloon bore The Castle's logo. The super-sized gift sat on an end table, Shaz didn't recognize.

His heart swelled as he walked forward and opened the card. The only message inside was, *We are family, Kings of the Castle*

Camilla eased her arm around him and rested her head on his shoulder. "It's beautiful. Where did it come from?"

Over the time they were together, she'd met only a few of his brothers. Yesterday, when they came to the hospital, she'd been too frazzled to assimilate everything. Now, he explained that the whole shebang was from the managing directors.

Camilla's eyes were moist when she said, "Tell them thanks for me."

"I will," he whispered, homing in on her lips. Camilla wrapped her arms around him and delved into the kiss as if she forgot they had an audience.

Martin's voice brought Shaz out of the fog he'd fallen into. "I'd tell the two of you to get a room, but you're in your own place."

Shaz lifted his head, still focused on Camilla. "That's right."

While Camilla blushed, Shaz greeted his blood brothers, who'd just arrived.

Dinner was a light-hearted affair with the family spread throughout the kitchen and living room. Even Miss Mabel turned up after work to make much of Camilla and Ayanna. After several hours, their guests trickled out until the three occupants were left in the suite.

* * *

Much later that night, when Ayanna was worn out from the excitement of the impromptu dinner party, Shaz lay with Camilla in his arms. Their skin was slick with sweat and when he got his breath back, he turned on his side to study her in the light coming from the bathroom. With lazy strokes, he trailed one finger over her stomach. "So, when d'you plan to make an honest man out of me?"

"Is that your idea of a marriage proposal, Shastra Bostwick?"

He chuckled and ran the pad of his thumb around her navel. "No, but I do have a thing or three in mind to make it something you won't soon forget."

"On that note ... " Camilla grabbed his wrist to still his hand. "What about the woman you were seeing before me? Or anyone else for that matter. I didn't think to ask."

He pulled her closer and looked her in the eyes. "What's in my past stays there. You're my future, Camilla Gibson."

With the back of her fingers, she grazed the hairs on his jaw. "Good, because I'm not planning on taking any 'bun' from you."

Laughing, Shaz relaxed his hold. "Your accent came out in full force just now when you mentioned me cheating." He reeled her in with one arm around her neck. "Trust me. I won't give you any 'bun'. I'm a one-woman kinda guy. Besides, my mother would kill me if I hurt you."

"I hope you remember that in one, five, ten, and twenty years from now."

"I'm not likely to forget," he said, "I'll be busy satisfying this insatiable appetite you have for me."

A low, sexy chuckle emerged from her throat. "You know the thing I love about you?"

He nuzzled her neck. "Well, there is a lot you could choose from, but I'm listening."

"You have such a big head," she said, gasping as his lips trailed across the tip of her breast. "All of that confidence must be good for something."

"That's it?" he asked, amused.

"Um, maybe if you stop what you're doing I could get my thoughts together."

"Ya think?"

When his fingers replaced his mouth, Camilla trembled. "Shaz, you have to …"

Hiding a smile, he whispered, "I don't *have to* do anything, but you were going to tell me something at least a half hour ago."

"Liar." She held his head between her hands. "I was saying … your generosity of spirit, your determination, the way you take care of me. Your acceptance of Ayanna." Her voice dropped to a whisper. "Thank you."

"No. *Thank you*," Shaz said against her neck. "Despite everything, you were a trooper. Stubborn, but willing to listen to me … eventually. Willing to let me lead. I love that." Holding her gaze, he added. "And I love you."

Her eyes were awash with tears when she blinked and cleared her throat. "Shastra Bostwick, I can't even begin to tell you the many ways in which I love and appreciate you."

A satisfied smile covered his face, then turned into a grin. "Look at it this way, you have a lifetime to show me."

"Uh-huh." Wearing a sneaky smile, Camilla slid a hand down his stomach, letting her fingers skim his rock-hard abs. "How about if I start right now?"

Heat spread everywhere Camilla left a gentle trail and after a moment, Shaz repositioned her next to him. "If this is what it's going to be, you're more than welcome to start as you mean to go on."

Camilla giggled and wrapped her fingers around him, pulling a gasp from deep in his throat. Shaz opened his mouth, but the only sound that emerged was a long moan.

The only answer in the room, for some time, was Camilla's soft answering cries.

GRUDGE

Through Shaz's interaction with his Jamaican cousin, you, dear reader were introduced to Phillip Denham, an officer in the Jamaican police force. He is as determined and tenacious as Shaz and his story is told in the romantic suspense novel, *Grudge*.

Blurb

After dumping her cheating ex, Corra Bingham goes on vacation to take her mind off the double whammy of the devastating betrayal and her overbearing father. But things turn complicated when she nearly loses her life to a ruthless and persistent stalker.

She's clueless as to why anyone would choose her for blood sport, but isn't happy when Phillip Denham appoints himself as her protector. He's everything she doesn't want in a man—good-looking, frugal with the truth, and a law-enforcement officer. Try as she might, she cannot make him go away.

On a previous visit to the exotic island of Xantrope, Phillip Denham discovered that he has a twin. His life is a complex web of lies and he wants answers. Intrigued by the missing pieces of his past, Phillip returns to the island to trace his roots.

While there, he encounters Corra and someone who is intent on putting her six feet under. She's a fascinating woman, but her relentless enemy makes him wonder what she's involved in. Using his skills as a detective, he races to find answers that will prevent Corra from ending up on a slab in the morgue.

J. L. Campbell

National Bestselling Author, J.L. Campbell writes contemporary, paranormal, and sweet romance, romantic suspense, women's fiction, as well as new and young adult novels.

Campbell, who features Jamaican culture in her stories, has penned over thirty books. She is a certified editor, who also writes non-fiction. When she's not writing, Campbell adds to her extensive collection of photos detailing Jamaica's flora and fauna. Visit her on the web at www.joylcampbell.com

Romantic Suspense (Island Adventure Series)
Anya's Wish (free novella)
Chasing Anya
Contraband
Taming Celeste
Grudge
Hardware

New Adult
Perfection
Fixation
Persuasion

Women's Fiction
A Baker's Dozen-13 Steps to Distraction (novella)
Dissolution
Distraction
Retribution
Absolution

The Thick of Things
The Heart of Things

Young Adult
Christine's Odyssey
Saving Sam

Short Story Collections
Don't Get Mad...Get Even (free)
Don't Get Mad...Get Even: Kicked to the Kerb

Contemporary Romance (Sweet Holiday Series)
The Vet's Christmas Pet
The Vet's Valentine Gift
The Vet's Secret Wish
Sold! (Relative Ties Book 1)
Cupid's Gift
Blindsided

Contemporary Romance
The Short Game (Par-For-The-Course) Book 1
The Long Game (Par-For-The-Course) Book 2
The Blind Shot (Par-For-The-Course) Book 3
The Spice of Life
Forever Mine

Paranormal Romance
Phantasm

ABOUT THE KINGS OF THE CASTLE SERIES

Books 2-9 are standalones, no cliffhangers, and can be read in any order.

Book 1 – Kings of the Castle, the introduction to the series and story of King of Wilmette (Vikkas Germaine)

USA TODAY, *New York Times*, and National Bestselling Authors work together to provide you with a world you'll never want to leave. The Castle. Powerful men unexpectedly brought together by their pasts and current circumstances will become a force to be reckoned with. Their combined efforts to find the people responsible for the attempt on their mentor's life, is the beginning of dangerous challenges that will alter the path of their lives forever. Not to mention, they will also draw the ire and deadly intent of current Castle members who wield major influence across the globe.

Fate made them brothers, but protecting the Castle and the women they love, will make them Kings.

www.thekingsofthecastle.com

King of Chatham - Book 2

While Mariano "Reno" DeLuca uses his skills and resources to create safe havens for battered women, a surge in criminal activity within the Chatham area threatens the women's anonymity and security. When Zuri, an exotic Tanzanian Princess, arrives seeking refuge from an arranged marriage and its deadly consequences, Reno is now forced to relocate the women in the shelter, fend off unforeseen enemies of The Castle, and endeavor not to lose his heart to the mysterious woman.

King of Evanston - Book 3

Raised as an immigrant, Shaz Bostwick knows the heartache of family separation firsthand. His personal goals and business ethics collide when a vulnerable woman stands to lose her baby in an underhanded and profitable scheme crafted by powerful, ruthless businessmen and politicians who have nefarious ties to The Castle. Shaz and the Kings of the Castle collaborate to uproot the dark forces intent on changing the balance of power within The Castle and destroying their mentor. National Bestselling Author, J.L. Campbell presents book 3 in the Kings of the Castle Series, featuring Shaz Bostwick.

King of Devon - Book 4

When a coma patient becomes pregnant, Jaidev Maharaj's medical facility comes under a government microscope and media scrutiny. In the midst of the investigation, he receives a mysterious call from someone in his past that demands that more of him than he's ever been willing to give and is made aware of a dark family secret that will destroy the people he loves most.

King of Morgan Park - Book 5

Two things threaten to destroy several areas of Daron Kincaid's life— the tracking device he developed to locate victims of sex trafficking and an inherited membership in a mysterious outfit called The Castle. The new developments set the stage to dismantle the relationship with a woman who's been trained to make men weak or put them on the other side of the grave. The secrets Daron keeps from Cameron and his inner circle only complicates an already tumultuous situation caused by an FBI sting that brought down his former enemies. Can Daron take on his enemies, manage his secrets and loyalty to the Castle without permanently losing the woman he loves?

King of South Shore - Book 6

Award-winning real estate developer, Kaleb Valentine, is known for turning failing communities into thriving havens in the Metro Detroit area. His plans to rebuild his hometown neighborhood are dereailed with one phone call that puts Kaleb deep in the middle of an intense criminal investigation led by a detective who has a personal vendetta. Now he will have to deal with the ghosts of his past before they kill him.

King of Lincoln Park - Book 7

Grant Khambrel is a sexy, successful architect with big plans to expand his Texas Company. Unfortunately, a dark secret from his past could destroy it all unless he's willing to betray the man responsible for that success, and the woman who becomes the key to his salvation.

King of Hyde Park - Book 8

Alejandro "Dro" Reyes has been a "fixer" for as long as he could remember, which makes owning a crisis management company focused on repairing professional reputations the perfect fit. The same could be said of Lola Samuels, who is only vaguely aware of his "true" talents and seems to be oblivious to the growing attraction between them. His company, Vantage Point, is in high demand and business in the Windy City is booming. Until a mysterious call following an attempt on his mentor's life forces him to drop everything and accept a fated position with The Castle. But there's a hidden agenda and unexpected enemy that Alejandro doesn't see coming who threatens his life, his woman, and his throne.

King of Lawndale - Book 9

Dwayne Harper's passion is giving disadvantaged boys the tools to transform themselves into successful men. Unfortunately, the minute he steps up to take his place among the men he considers brothers, two things stand in his way: a political office that does not want the competition Dwayne's new education system will bring, and a well-connected former member of The Castle who will use everything in his power—even those who Dwayne mentors—to shut him down.

AUTHOR BIOS

Naleighna Kai is the *USA TODAY* Bestselling Author of Every Woman Needs a Wife, Open Door Marriage, Loving Me for Me, Slaves of Heaven and several other controversial novels. She is founder of NK Tribe Called Success, The Cavalcade of Authors, and is a publishing and marketing consultant. www.naleighnakai.com

S. L. Jennings is a military wife, mom of three, coffee addict, Willy Wonka enthusiast, and real-life unicorn. She's also the New York Times and USA Today Bestselling author of Taint, Fear of Falling and the Se7en Sinners Series, along with a few other titles that she's too lazy to type. She's been with her high school sweetheart for almost twenty years, and he still can't get her Subway sandwich order right. But he's cute and brings her vodka, so she keeps him around. They currently reside in Spokane, WA with their three stinky boys and their equally stinky cat. www.sljenningsauthor.com

Martha Kennerson is the bestselling and award-winning author who's love of reading and writing is a significant part of who she is. She uses both to create the kinds of stories that touch the heart. Martha lives with her family in League City, Texas. She believes her current blessings are only matched by the struggle it took to achieve such happiness. To find out more about Martha and her journey, visit her website at www. marthakennerson.com and you can follow her on Facebook and Twitter.

J. L. Campbell is an award-winning Jamaican author who has written over thirty books in several romance subgenres. Campbell, who features Jamaican culture in her stories, is a certified editor, and also writes non-fiction. Visit her on the web at www.joylcampbell.com.

National bestselling author, **Lisa Watson**, is a native of Washington D.C., and writes in the Multicultural & Interracial, Contemporary, Romantic Suspense, and Sweet Romance genres. Her memorable novels for the Harlequin's Kimani line, The Match Broker series was listed as one of 2014's Top 25 Books of the Summer, and Top 50 Best Reads. Lisa lives in Raleigh, North Carolina with her husband of twenty-two years and two teenagers, and is avidly working on book one, Alexa King: The Guardian, in her second new Romantic Suspense series, The Lady Doyen and Book 2 in the Love and Danger Series. www.lisawatson.com

Karen D. Bradley is a national bestselling author and screenplay writer. English and Grammar were never her strongest subjects, but as life would have it, her weakest link would become her saving grace. Writing fiction became one of her favorite forms of therapy. She has penned several contemporary fiction, suspense, and romantic suspense novels. Visit Karen on the web at www.karendbradley.com

Janice M. Allen is a National Bestselling Author who has always been an avid reader of fiction. She even edited the work of other authors for several years. But she gets an incomparable thrill from creating stories that entertain readers and cause them to reflect on real life issues. No Right Way To Do A Wrong Thing is her first novel, followed by her short story Cayenne. www.janicemallen.com

London St. Charles has always had a passion for the pen, paper, and books. She is a Chicago native who uses the Windy City as a backdrop to the romance, suspense, and contemporary fiction stories she writes. London published her debut novel, The Husband We Share in 2017 and is one of nine authors in the anthology, Sugar. She also composes an online newsletter, London Writes, that keeps readers abreast of what's going on in her world. www.londonstcharles.com

MarZe Scott is a lifelong resident of Ypsilanti, Michigan and Graduate of University of Michigan. A lover of all things creative, MarZé enjoys reading, free-hand illustrating, jewelry making and makeup artistry.

Known for her vivid and captivating storytelling, MarZé has been writing short stories and poems since elementary school and developed a taste in high school for writing about provocative topics like the consequences of casual sex. You can find Gemini Rising, MarZé's debut novel, and short story Next Lifetime wherever books are sold. www.marzescott.com

SERIES MENTORS:

LaVerne Thompson is a *USA Today* Bestselling, award winning, multi-published author, an avid reader and a writer of contemporary, fantasy, and sci/fi sensual romances. She loves creating worlds within and without our world. She also writes romantic suspense and new adult romance under the pen name Ursula Sinclair also a USA Today Bestselling Author. www.lavernethompson.com

Kassanna is a strong believer in love at first sight and happily ever afters. Writing has always been her passion but fate sometimes has other roads that must first be taken .Navigating the road less traveled was not only unexpected but in the end extremely rewarding. Her books are mainly contemporary romance but she has delved into the paranormal, fantasy, and plans on expanding into other areas as the ideas come to her. Right now she is enjoying life and seeing her works come into fruition make it that much more pleasurable especially when her books make others smile. Kassanna wouldn't have it any other way. www.flavorfullove.com

The Long Game (Par for the Course - Book 1)

One kiss. Two friends. Three relationships changed.

Garth Chu owns the most sought-after video production outfit in Kingston, Jamaica. Everything is lining up well, including his relationship. That's until his mother tries to bulldoze him into marrying a woman of their ethnicity. And things get even stickier when his girl, Nadine, joins the crusade to get Garth to propose.

Anna-Lise Myers has been Garth's golfing buddy for fifteen years and resents Nadine's intrusion on their friendship. When Garth is injured in an accident, things take an unexpected turn. Anna-Lise discovers feelings she's never admitted to having and Garth can't remember when Anna-Lise went from sister-friend to potential lady-love.

A sensuous interlude forces them to decide whether they want to risk their friendship and take a chance on happy-ever-after.

The Short Game (Par for the Course - Book 2)

He's all she's ever wanted. She's all he'll ever need.

Aside from a brief stint of madness during their teen years, Vance and Ayisha are not each other's idea of relationship material. Vance is preoccupied with getting his fill of women. Yet, all it takes to turn his world upside down is one remark from Ayisha about his lifestyle.

Suddenly, his focus shifts and he's spending his days trying to prove he can be the man she needs. While he's intent on leaving his player days behind, an unseen enemy is determined to ruin his career as a financial analyst.

Ayisha is a go-getter who knows what she's about—a successful business, a lifetime with the man of her dreams, and children to complete the picture. Vance is an expert at romance, but with Ayisha it's all or nothing. She's waited years for him to stop chasing the wind in pursuit of what's already in front of him. Now that he's set his heart on having her, will she accept his love?

The Blind Shot (Par for the Course - Book 3)

When all else fails, love will find a way.

Kofi Danquah has traveled halfway around the globe for fifteen years, satisfying his need for advancement and adventure. In that time, he has never met another woman as intriguing as Regina Chu. She's a chameleon—a wild child with issues she hides behind a playful persona.

In Gina's eyes, Kofi is a mystery—exotic, intense and secretive. His sober nature balances her bubbly personality and unconventional approach to life. Plus, he's appealing enough to make her forget they're from separate worlds.

Time spent together changes Kofi and Gina's platonic relationship into an attraction that burns hot despite their cultural differences and the disapproval of their families. But fairy tales don't always last and true love needs fertile soil in which to bloom.

**** The Blind Shot contains the potential trigger subject of date rape.* While the incident isn't shown on the page, this warning may be helpful to those readers who may be affected by that subject matter.

* 9 7 8 9 7 6 9 5 5 8 6 7 0 *